RECOLLECTIONS OF SOCRATES

and

SOCRATES' DEFENSE
BEFORE THE JURY

The Library of Liberal Arts

OSKAR PIEST, FOUNDER

RECOLLECTIONS OF SOCRATES

and

SOCRATES' DEFENSE
BEFORE THE JURY

Xenophon

Translated, with an Introduction, by
Anna S. Benjamin
Professor of Classics, Rutgers University

The Library of Liberal Arts
published by
THE BOBBS-MERRILL COMPANY, INC.
A Subsidiary of Howard W. Sams & Co., Inc.
Publishers • Indianapolis • New York • Kansas City

Xenophon: 426–354 B.C.

Copyright © 1965
THE BOBBS-MERRILL COMPANY, INC.
Printed in the United States of America
Library of Congress Catalog Card Number 64-66080
First Printing

CONTENTS

INTRODUCTION

Socrates and Athens and the Year 399 B.C.

Recollections of Socrates and *Socrates' Defense Before the Jury* record one of those rare occasions in history when a moment, forced into a crisis, rolls relentlessly toward an overwhelming question. The men who forced the moment into crisis were Socrates, the prosecutors who brought him to trial, and the Athenians who judged him. The question posed was how much intellectual freedom can a state allow its citizens; the answer, devised for the occasion, appears to be a brutal denial of individual freedom, an act of terrorism, for Socrates was put to death. Because the issues of the crisis of 399 B.C. have never ceased to haunt civilized society and sovereign states, later generations have ever been drawn to examine the events of this crucial year. For their study, the two works by Xenophon here translated are among the major documents available. They were written as a result of the furor that arose around Socrates' life and death, and they attempt to explain what happened, why it happened, and what Socrates was like.

Athens in the Age of Pericles, in contrast to other centers of culture at the time, provided a freedom for intellectual activity and discussion that attracted thinkers from all over the ancient world. The atmosphere of the city nourished debate, experiment, and creative activity in all the arts. Witness to the extraordinary measure of this freedom may be found in all of the arts and fields of knowledge pursued at the time, but perhaps the most striking testimony is the license of Greek comedy, in which political, intellectual, and literary figures are mercilessly lampooned.[1] As one of the most productive and

[1] However, the court proceedings against Pericles' friends, such as Anaxagoras the philosopher and the artist Phidias, attest to the influential element in Athens that sought to restrain this freedom.

inventive eras in the memory of man, the fifth century in Athens provides a remarkable illustration of the coincidence of intellectual and political freedom. Not only did these freedoms accompany each other, but they were so interfused that the realms of thought and action were not incompatible, and the leading thinkers of the day could find a place for their energies in politics and business. The fusion of these two realms found its material expression in the Athenian agora, the setting of both of Xenophon's works. Here was the center of the intellectual life of the city as well as the seat of Athenian democracy and commerce. Here all of the government bureaus were housed, the public notices posted, the laws published, the courts convened; here goods from around the world were bought and sold, the financial and banking interests of the Athenian empire energetically protected. The agora was the setting for the men—whoever they might be— who had something to say, to ask, to teach, or to learn. Here these men met Socrates (469–399 B.C.), an Athenian citizen, registered as the son of Sophroniscus and Phaenarete in the deme of Alopece, Attica. Many came expressly to talk to him, many merely chanced upon him and lingered, many he sought out. In his eagerness to talk, he did not even take the time to practice the trade of stone-cutting he had learned from his father. His life was bound to the agora at Athens, and indeed he rarely left the city except to fight for his fatherland (at Potidaea, 432 B.C.; Delium, 424 B.C.; Amphipolis, 422 B.C.) and possibly for pilgrimages to the Isthmus and to Delphi. A cross section of the men who, in the heart of commercial and political Athens, found time to talk with Socrates is presented in the *Recollections*. Of the sophists with whom Socrates steadfastly refused to identify himself, Xenophon introduces two: Hippias of Elis and Antiphon. True to the characteristics Plato ascribes to sophists, they are hostile to Socrates; Antiphon is patronizingly sympathetic about Socrates' poverty, and Hippias eager to force Socrates, whom he considers limited and repetitive, to say something definite. Aristippus of Cyrene and Antisthenes discuss self-control and friendship—topics important to the doctrines they propounded when they later became identified with philosophical schools of their own. Prominent politicians seek Socrates out; Critias and Charicles attempt to threaten him into silence, only to be drawn into a long conversation and to be goaded into an angry revelation of their real motives. The younger Pericles bemoans the decline of Athens with Socrates, and most good-naturedly accepts the lessons he offers. Political nonentities like Nicomachides are made to rethink their standards for office-holding. The family of Plato meets Socrates at the agora: Glaucon, Plato's brother, to discover the dangers of premature entry into politics, and Charmides, Plato's uncle, to discover that his reluctance to enter politics is unjustified. Socrates' oldest and most intimate friend, Crito, is advised to befriend Archedemus. Aristodemus, Chaerecrates, and Hermogenes, three faithful companions of Socrates, the armor maker Pistias, the painter Parrhasius, the high-class prostitute Theodote, the businessmen Aristarchus and Eutherus—all attest to the fascination of the man and the diversity of his conversation. He is busy dealing with the men who ran Athenian affairs, prodding them about such great issues as "What is just, lawful, or good?" as well as about trivia like table manners. He humiliates some, encourages others.

In placing him in the agora among men of all callings and classes, Xenophon reveals a Socrates who is both a man of affairs and a philosopher. His activities, however, came to an end in 399 B.C. when, with an explosion of angry charges and swift hatred, the freedom that Athens had provided Socrates vanished in a court arraignment on the charge of corrupting the youth of Athens and of irreverence to the gods of the state. The jury found him guilty by a vote of 281 to 220. When, according to Athenian law, he was given an opportunity to propose for the jury's consideration a counter-penalty in place of death, he astounded the court by pointing out that he really deserved, not a penalty, but honor. Plato records that he offered to pay a fine of 30 minae, while Xenophon states that he refused to propose a counter-penalty at all.

At any rate, the jury was so outraged that eighty who had previously voted "not guilty" shifted their vote, and Socrates was sentenced to death and executed. His execution marks the moment when the Athenian intellectuals withdrew from the mainstream of Athenian affairs to form separate schools. From that time on, the chasm between the realm of thought and that of action was rarely bridged in Athens.

The figure of Socrates and the judgment of the Athenian jurors upon him generated a controversy which, fed by the dearth of first-hand knowledge about him, still commands man's attention and best powers of speculation. The focus of the controversy is the double question of who Socrates was and what he was like. The discrepancy between the fact of his condemnation and the fact of his profound effect in Athens is striking. Through the men he taught—Plato, for one—Socrates revolutionized Greek thought and exerted an influence which is still active today.[2] But what was he really like, that the Athenians put him to death? Were they justified? Was his influence really for evil, as the judgment implies? Has posterity been duped by a hoax into regarding Socrates as a noble thinker martyred by his contemporaries? Or, if the judgment was a mistake, how could the jurors have been so misguided?

In his lifetime, Socrates was a legend that attracted to Athens the leading intellectuals of the ancient world; upon his death the legend grew, as men tried to resolve the problems. There are no official records or first-hand documents, acceptable to modern historical standards, about the trial; and Socrates wrote nothing, or virtually nothing.[3] What is known

---

[2] The term "Socratic revolution" is applied to the new direction toward ethics and the new orientation toward value that Greek thought took under Socrates' influence. Aristotle (*Metaphysics* XIII. 4. 3–5, 1078b 17–32) sums up Socrates' contribution to Greek philosophy by pointing out that Socrates turned his attention toward moral virtues and was the first to try to define them, and by ascribing to him two advances in dialectic: inductive reasoning and general definition.

[3] An Aristeides of the second century after Christ mentions letters of Socrates, and Plato in the *Phaedo* depicts him composing poetry while awaiting his execution.

of him is derived largely from the partisan writings of his two younger contemporaries, Plato (*ca.* 427–347 B.C.) and Xenophon (*ca.* 426–*ca.* 354 B.C.), both of whom wrote openly in his defense. One bitter contemporary attack on Socrates does exist: a comedy, *The Clouds,* presented by Aristophanes in 423 B.C., in which Socrates is represented as a sophist who quibbles over words, undermines morals and the state by his teachings, and trains the young to question the authority of parents and state. This satirical picture embodies a point of view about Socrates that many of his contemporaries must have had, although it is hard to reconcile with the fact that even in the works of the pro-Socratic Plato, Aristophanes is represented as being on good terms with Socrates.

Socratic Literature and Xenophon

Although much of the wealth of literature focused upon Socrates is lost, Xenophon's works have preserved for us three types of Socratic writings. The first is a new literary genre that came into being because of Socrates, although paradoxically he himself wrote nothing: the *Sokratikoi logoi,* or Socratic dialogue in prose, best represented by the dialogues of Plato and Xenophon in which Socrates appears as an interlocutor. They purport to be the words spoken by Socrates with his friends or enemies, but as Plato indicates by often making his dialogues second- and third-hand accounts of conversations, they cannot be construed as verbatim records of what was said. Xenophon wrote two Socratic dialogues which are obviously fictional: the *Economics* and the *Symposium.* The *Economics* deals with theories of estate management placed in the mouth of Socrates (a device that Plato, too, employed to present his own doctrines). The *Symposium* pretends to give an eyewitness account of a banquet attended by Socrates, Xenophon, and others in 421 B.C. Since Xenophon was only six or seven years old at the time, the pretense of historical truth must be judged to be a literary device. In its early form, the new prose genre was limited to dialogues in which Socrates participated; but soon it developed into a major form for philosophical treatises in the ancient world, and it has continued to reappear throughout Western literature.

The second literary genre represented in extant Socratic literature is the defense speech—the apology, to use the time-honored term that has only recently become obsolete. Because of the furor created by Socrates' trial, a good many of these defense speeches circulated soon after the event, and since Socrates' actual words in court are not known from official records, the tradition about the events of the trial lies embedded in the apologetic literature. The four extant defenses are: Plato's *Apology,* which purports to be Socrates' speech in court (Plato says that he was present at the trial); the defense included by Xenophon in the *Recollections of Socrates* (I. 1–2 and IV. 8); Xenophon's *Socrates' Defense Before the Jury;*[4] and Libanius' *Apology,* written in the fifth century after Christ, a literary fiction (as indeed they all may be!) based on the scholar's readings in the Socratic tradition. Comparisons of the defenses by Socrates' contemporaries, Plato and Xenophon, have led to the most diverse results and to every conceivable conclusion about their interdependence or lack of dependence—from theories that Plato composed his *Apology* after Xenophon wrote his, to hypotheses that Xenophon has written merely a mediocre imitation of the Platonic defense. Even the relation between Xenophon's two defenses cannot be determined: *Socrates' Defense Before the Jury* appears to be an earlier defense expanded later in the *Recollections.* But again, it may be just the reverse, a summary. There is simply not enough evidence to establish facts about the dates and interrelationships of the Platonic and Xenophontic defenses. Theories about Socrates that rely on decisions about the prior-

---

[4] Doubts about Xenophon's authorship of this defense ignore the weighty evidence that there is no known record of similar doubts in antiquity and that Diogenes Laertius, who often records debates over authorship in his biographies, lists this work among the genuine works of Xenophon.

ity and dependence of one work upon another can be at most only probable. For later generations it is the legend of Socrates that is important, as it sheds light upon the ancient world and as it grew continuously through the course of Western thought, and is still developing. The facts about Socrates' defense remain for the most part lost. The legend, however, is available; to fail to explore one or another part of it on the basis that it does not appear to be fact is to ignore a revelation about ancient culture and Socrates' influence on it, if not about Socrates himself.

Socrates' Defense Before the Jury, as related by Xenophon, includes features that set it apart from the other apologies. First of all, Xenophon, who was away during the period of Socrates' trial and execution, states that he draws upon a certain Hermogenes for his information about Socrates' last days. Hermogenes was a friend of Socrates, and appears in the *Recollections.*[5] He was a follower of the Cynic philosopher Antisthenes—a fact which may well account for the emphasis in the *Defense* (sections 6–7) on Socrates' views on death, which are akin to doctrines of the Cynic school. Inquiry as to when and how Hermogenes communicated his information to Xenophon, or whether Xenophon merely read Hermogenes' account in a written defense, leads nowhere and again is not sufficient reason to set aside the work when considering Socrates. Secondly, in his apology, Xenophon states that he has written to supplement and correct other accounts of Socrates' defense; he admits in section 22 that his version is not complete. The main point that Xenophon makes which he thinks has been ignored in other defense speeches is the reason for the grandiloquent manner of speaking (*megalegoría*) Socrates employed before the jury. Others had noticed, he observed, this grandiloquence, but they did not explain that the reason for it was that Socrates considered death at this time preferable to life—a simple but rather disappointing motivation, to the modern reader schooled in psychological complexity.

[5] II. 10. 3–6, I. 2. 48, IV. 8. 4; and possibly he is the impoverished friend alluded to in II. 5. 3–4.

Third, unlike Plato's *Apology*, Xenophon's is not in the form of a speech; rather, it takes up certain high points of Socrates' last days, such as his *megalegoria* and his refusal to prepare a formal defense speech for the trial. It quotes part of Socrates' refutation of the charges of impiety and corruption of the youth, and a solemn charge that Socrates made to the jury after it voted the death penalty for him. Xenophon closes his work with an account of the events occurring after the trial and before Socrates' execution. These features show that Socrates' manner of presenting his defense was peculiar by the standards of his day, and not what was expected. They imply too that Socrates did not actually prepare a text in his own defense. Furthermore, by emphasizing his sources, Xenophon is trying to make his reader believe that he, in contrast to other writers, is presenting the "real" Socrates. The controversy over the trial was already active this early!

The extant apologies imply the existence of a body of anti-Socratic writings that attack Socrates and defend the action of the court. The court speeches of the three prosecutors who brought the formal charges recorded by Xenophon and Plato against Socrates have not been preserved. Anytus, Meletus, and Lycon are the three Athenians whose names are for all time associated with the trial, and with little else. Meletus was the chief prosecutor, with the other two as co-prosecutors, although Anytus was the most important and influential of the three: he had served Athens as general, was politically allied with the popular party and a vigorous opponent of the oligarchy. Lycon is known only as a youthful aristocrat lampooned in comedy. While the court speeches are lost, traces of a later anti-Socratic pamphlet of 393 or 392 B.C. by a now almost unknown Athenian orator, Polycrates, a partisan of radical democracy who flourished in the early fourth century before Christ, may be reconstructed from the first book of Xenophon's *Recollections* (I. 2. 9–61), where charges of "the prosecutor" are answered, and from the *Apology* of Libanius. Libanius' work, based on the Socratic literature available to him, records the charges of Polycrates in long quotations, and then refutes them. These traces of Polycrates' pamphlet are of great importance in understanding why Socrates was brought to trial, for they make very explicit the strong political motives of his opposition.[6] In his attack, Polycrates placed Socrates in the oligarchical party and pictured him as a teacher of young oligarchs like Critias, who employed the worst methods of terrorism during his political supremacy in 404–403 B.C. He held Socrates responsible for the political treachery and the immorality of Alcibiades. To give his attack an even sharper barb, Polycrates reminded Athenians that great democrats of old, like Miltiades and Themistocles, had never studied with philosophers. Polycrates accused Socrates of shirking his political responsibilities and of teaching anti-democratic interpretations of the poets Hesiod and Homer. None of these political charges could be used openly in the trial of 399 B.C. because the courts in Athens were still operating under the terms of the political amnesty of 403, which forbade lawsuits for political activities. Yet the swiftly flowing political undercurrent of Socrates' trial makes more comprehensible the motives of the jurors' judgment, and the severity of the penalty they pronounced.

The third literary genre represented in Xenophon's Socratic writings is that of *apomnemoneumata* ("recollections" or "records"): collections of sayings and deeds ascribed to a master and collected by his disciples. Xenophon's *Recollections of Socrates* are the earliest extant recollections in Western literature; the genre is best known through the collections made by Christ's disciples and contained in the New Testament. The Greek word *apomnemoneumata* means simply "recollections," but in the Renaissance the title was translated by Lenklau (Leonclavius) in his Latin translation of 1596 as *Memorabilia* ("things worth remembering"), and this is the title most frequently used.[7]

---

[6] These political motives are quite explicit in the Platonic dialogues, e.g., *Gorgias*, but are frequently overlooked because of the emphasis on the philosophical issues.

[7] The accurate Latin translation of *apomnemoneumata* is *commentarii*.

The *Memorabilia* (to use the shorter title) is close to biography in spirit: Xenophon claims to present the historical Socrates, although he does not detail systematically, from birth to death, the sequence of events in Socrates' life. He begins with a two-chapter defense of Socrates, which amounts to a proof that the Athenian jurors made an unjust judgment; expressing wonder at their decision, he explains that in several cases the jurors must have misunderstood the sayings of Socrates, especially his claims to be guided by a *daimon* [8] and his interpretations of the poets. Xenophon's defense is free from any outright denunciations of the jurors who sentenced Socrates to death; they are more subtly and effectively condemned as Xenophon allows the portrait he creates to imply how great was the miscarriage of justice in the Athenian court. The recollections themselves begin with the third chapter, and the statement:

> Inasmuch as Socrates was, I believe, useful to his associates, both through his actions in which he revealed what he was like and through the discussions he held, I shall now write what I recollect of these words and deeds.

In the variety of unrelated conversations that follow, and among the many people who appear, the unifying theme is Socrates himself as benefactor of Athens and of the men he met. The *Memorabilia* closes with a chapter on the death of Socrates, and a brief eulogy.

Xenophon's statement "I shall now write what I recollect . . ." cannot be taken to mean that he is recording verbatim what he witnessed and heard. There are indications that Xenophon's pretended presence at these conversations is simply a literary device to enhance the historical truth of

---

[8] Socrates' *daimon* or *daimonion* appears to have been a divine voice that at times warned Socrates not to do certain things. That Socrates claimed to have received these warnings is related by Xenophon and by Plato (*Phaedrus* 242b; *Apology* 31d, 40a; *Euthyphro* 3b, and many other passages). His contemporaries were mystified, curious, and even indignant about Socrates' divine voice, and in later antiquity writers like Plutarch and Apuleius continued to speculate on its nature.

his Socrates.[9] We have several reasons for hesitating to accept his statement as meaning that he is presenting an eyewitness account: Xenophon's association with Socrates was brief and confined to his youthful years. All indications point to his having closely attended upon Socrates only between 403 and his departure from Athens in 401. And since Xenophon did not return until 365, his relationship with Socrates' Athenian followers was also curtailed. It is, as well, hard to imagine Xenophon as a silent bystander in so many conversations, especially when they were as private and personal as that between Socrates and his own son (II. 2) or with Chaerecrates about his brother (II. 3). It is equally difficult to assume that he made notes on so many conversations, even if he could have heard them all. Again, some of the opinions expressed by Socrates seem to be the opinions of others put into the mouth of Socrates, such as his discourse on self-control (I. 2. 1) or his refusal to take money for fear of losing his freedom (I. 2. 6–7), both of which might well be the Cynic doctrines of Antisthenes. Xenophon appears to be using the character of Socrates as he did in the *Economics,* to propound his own theories and interests, especially when he liberally praises Sparta or discusses the duties of a cavalry officer or hunting or horsemanship—subjects on which he himself wrote treatises. He could have known Socrates well enough to draw heavily on his own personal recollections, and he may well have written notes on things he heard. The analogy to his method in writing the *Anabasis,* where he drew on personal experience, adds to the probability that Xenophon's picture is based on personal contact, but that he has also drawn from other writings, or informants, or both—although who or what they may be is only conjecture. His declared intention is to write of the Socrates he knows, and by mentioning several times that he was present

[9] Xenophon's historical veracity has been questioned in all of his historical writings. One instance is his claim in the *Anabasis* to be an important leader. He is not even mentioned in Diodorus Siculus' subsequent narrative (1st century B.C.) of the incident, but this fact is not in itself proof that Xenophon represented his own role as more important than it really was, since Diodorus' narrative is very much abbreviated.

at events he describes, he takes pains to try to maintain the atmosphere of historical truth. He weaves a net of historical plausibility around Socrates by introducing a host of Athenians and foreigners tied by numerous threads not only to Socrates and to each other, but also to the events and the setting of fifth-century Athens.

His picture becomes all the more convincing by means of his flowing prose, famous for its grace and elegance. *Balance, simplicity,* and *purity* are the words most often used in describing Xenophon's style: balance and simplicity in the order of words and in the construction; purity in diction. There is little that is extraneous or contrived in this straightforward reconstruction of Socrates' sayings and deeds.

Xenophon: Adventurer and Man of Letters

Xenophon (426–354 B.C.) [10] was one of the most energetic of Athenians. His adventurous life brought him friends and acquaintances from all over Greece and Persia, including politicians, writers, philosophers, and professional soldiers. He wrote on a variety of historical, political, and technical subjects. He fought in Asia and Europe; travel led him far into the Persian Empire and to many sections of the Greek world. His youth in Athens coincided with the restless end of the fifth century, when the city was involved in wars at home and aboard and torn by internal revolutions, siege, and enemy occupation. His conscription into military service probably came in the year that the Thirty Tyrants held power in Athens; he served under them in the cavalry. Their political intrigues occupy an important part of his history of Greece, the *Hellenica*—a fact which points to his lifelong pattern of drawing heavily upon first-hand experience in his writings; his experiences moved him to write. He is at one and the same time a writer and an adventurer.

Though neither Plato nor Aristotle lists Xenophon among

10 The dates are conjectural.

the followers of Socrates, the first notable event in his life un-
deniably connects him closely with Socrates: around 401 B.C.
a friend, Proxenus, invited him to join him at the court of
the Persian prince, Cyrus the Younger, in Sardis, Asia Minor.
The sway that Socrates exerted over Xenophon was so strong
that he went to Socrates for advice about whether to go. Socrates advised consulting the oracle at Delphi and, although
Socrates objected to the way Xenophon phrased his question
for the oracle—he asked *how*, not *whether*, he should go—Socrates advised him to leave Athens for Sardis. The year and a
half between his military service and his departure for Cyrus'
court must be the time when Xenophon fell under the spell
of Socrates, and is the period from which stem most of Xenophon's personal memories of Socrates. Certainly even as little
as a year is sufficient for a teacher and pupil to establish and
share the intensely close relationship by which a great teacher
dominates and changes the student's life. If Xenophon made
any notes at all on Socrates, they go back to these months at
the end of the century, although it was not until the appearance of Polycrates' attack that he publicly entered the controversy with his own reconstruction of what Socrates was like.
The decision to leave Athens brought Xenophon years of adventures, the first of which are recounted in his work entitled
the *Anabasis*, or *March Inland*, where he tells of his travels
(401–399) with the Greek mercenary troops that Cyrus had
hired to help him in a bid to seize the kingship in Persia. The
defeat and death of Cyrus in the Battle of Cunaxa (401 B.C.)
left the Greek troops stranded in hostile country; Xenophon
describes how the 10,000 mercenary troops marched through
hostile territory into the interior of Asia Minor, through the
upper regions of the Tigris, and around finally to the safety
of the Black Sea, where the friendly Greek colonies were located. When he left the mercenary troops, Xenophon stayed
in Asia Minor without returning to the city that had, during
his absence, put Socrates to death. He campaigned with the
Spartan forces led by the commander from Sparta, Dercyllides,
and the Spartan King Agesilaus.

Exile From Athens

Sometime during the first decade of the fourth century, Xenophon was exiled from Athens, apparently *in absentia,* because of his pro-Spartan sympathies; this exile seems to reflect a victory of the democratic party over the Athenian oligarchs, who were usually pro-Spartan. Xenophon in his writings does not indulge in recriminations or show open resentment against Athens, and his very genuine and open admiration for Spartan government and education is not tinged with bitterness. He lived most of his mature years outside of his native city, and even fought for Sparta against Athens and her allies at the Battle of Coronea (394 B.C.). His life away from Athens is echoed in the international tone of his writings and their focus upon Spartan leaders and institutions. The *Agesilaus* (written after the king's death in 360) is a eulogy and defense of the Spartan king; the *Constitution of Sparta* is a political treatise presenting a laudatory account of Spartan institutions; the *Education of Cyrus* (written after 365) presents an ideal Persian prince, Cyrus the Elder, who received a Spartan education; and the treatise *On Tyranny,* or the *Hiero* (358/7) is a dialogue on the institution of tyranny, placed in the mouths of the tyrant Hiero of Sicily and the poet Simonides.

During the 380's, Xenophon changed his way of life and settled with his family on an estate provided him by Sparta, to live the life of a country gentleman—caring for his property, hunting, writing, entertaining. Scillus is a small town in the Peloponnesus near Olympia, Elis; it was not isolated, for it was close to the great international shrine of the Olympian Zeus. From his Socratic dialogue, the *Economics,* the reader may surmise something of the life Xenophon led on his estate, and something of how he ran his affairs. Not only does the treatise contain information on farming and animal husbandry; there is also a large section devoted to how the mistress of the house may keep the home in such good order that upon her husband's request, she may quickly find everything—from boots to a work of art. Even advice to the mistress of the estate on make-up is not too trivial for Xenophon to mention. At Scillus, Xenophon built a small shrine to Artemis, modeled after the great shrine at Ephesus, and held yearly festivals to which many came from home and abroad.

The peaceful life at Scillus lasted into the next decade, but by 371, Xenophon was again on the move, and left his estate forever. The decree of exile was rescinded at Athens, and he returned home around 365 B.C. There he again turned his ever-practical interests to Athenian affairs, as we may judge from the treatise *On Revenues,* written after his return, in which he discusses the Athenian silver mines at Laurium as a neglected source of revenue for the state. Also at this time, he wrote his discussions of the duties of a cavalry officer, the *Hipparch;* and he continued his history of Greece to the year 362 B.C.

At his death (probably in 354) Xenophon left behind him one of the largest extant bodies of fourth-century Greek literature, highly admired in antiquity and much imitated; but from the nineteenth century on, his works have been dismissed by most critics as second-rate. These later generations seem to be unable to forgive Xenophon for not being Thucydides when he writes history, or Plato when he writes of Socrates. Not that comparison with these writers is unjust, or should not be made: in each case, Xenophon himself invited the comparison. In writing his history of Greece, the *Hellenica,* he set out to continue from where Thucydides left off (411) and adopted Thucydides' chronological format. In the case of his Socratic writings, he deliberately chose, as a self-appointed biographer, to enter the Socratic controversy with his own version of what Socrates was like. How Xenophon fares is a matter to be determined between each reader and Xenophon himself. He should be judged in terms of what he is: an adventurer and man of affairs, involved in the practical business of Greek domestic and international politics and war, and a practical man of the world who writes on philosophical, historical, and technical topics. In his treatise *On Hunting* he styles himself an amateur, and this self-portrait, whether he is posing or not, is the one that rings true. A fourth-century Odysseus, he wandered about the Greek and Persian world, an exile. His curiosity was voracious, his tolerance for adventure enormous. Unlike Odysseus, he found time to reflect on his adventures and on the people he met, and when he reflected, he distilled his reflections into writing. All of his wide experience and reading are brought to bear upon his writings, and the topics upon which he wrote and reflected were always timely; he had an unerring eye for the important issues of his times. His mingled Athenian, Persian, and Spartan interests, his life of adventure and of political and military opportunism, his interest in the philosophical, educational, and technical topics of the day, herald the new Greece formed after the collapse of Athens and her empire; they are part of the new spirit that found its culmination in Alexander's conquests and the reformation of the Greek world into an international culture.

NOTE ON THE TEXT: The translation is based on the text edited by E. G. Marchant in the Oxford Classical Text series, *Xenophontis Opera Omnia*, Volume II. 2nd edition, 1921; reprinted 1955.

BIBLIOGRAPHY

Xenophon's Extant Works

Historical Writings
Anabasis (Expeditio Cyri)
Hellenica (Historia Graeca)
Agesilaus

Political Writings[1]
The Constitution of Sparta
The Education of Cyrus (Cyropaedia)
Hiero or *On Tyranny*

Technical Treatises
On Hunting (Cynegeticus)
On Horsemanship (De re equestri)
The Hipparch (Hipparchus)
On Revenues (De vectigalibus)

Socratic Writings
Symposium
Economics (Oeconomicus)
Socrates' Defense Before the Jury (Apologia Socratis)
Recollections of Socrates (Memorabilia)

---

[1] *The Constitution of Athens,* sometimes attributed to Xenophon, is generally conceded to be spurious.

The following brief list includes works that present the major issues of the Socratic controversy and will lead to a complete bibliography upon the subject:

ARNIM, H. V. *Xenophons Memorabilien und Apologie des Socrates.* (Det Koneglig Danske Videnskabornes Selskab. "Historisk-filologiske Meddelelser," VIII, 1.) Copenhagen: Høst, 1923.

CHROUST, ANTON-HERMANN. *Socrates, Man and Myth: The Two Socratic Apologies of Xenophon.* London: Routledge & Kegan Paul, 1957.

DELATTE, A. *Le Troisième livre des souvenirs Socratiques de Xénophon.* (Bibliothèque de la faculté de philosophie et lettres de l'Université de Liège, LVIII.) Paris Librairie E. Droz, 1933.

DELEBEQUE, ÉDOUARD. *Essai sur la vie de Xénophon.* (Études et commentaires, XXV.) Paris: Klincksieck, 1957.

GIGON, OLOF. *Kommentar zum ersten Buch von Xenophons Memorabilien.* (Schweizerische Beiträge zur Altertumswissenschaft, Heft 5.) Basel: Verlag Friedrich Reinhardt, 1953.

———. *Kommentar zum zweiten Buch von Xenophons Memorabilien.* (Schweizerische Beiträge zur Altertumswissenschaft, Heft 7.) Basel: Verlag Friedrich Reinhardt, 1956.

GUARDINI, ROMANO. *The Death of Socrates, an Interpretation of the Platonic Dialogues: Euthyphro, Apology, Crito, and Phaedo.* Translated by BASIL WRIGHTON. New York: Sheed & Ward, 1948.

LONGO, V. *ΑΝΗΡ ΟΦΕΛΙΜΟΣ, Il problema della composizione dei "Memorabili di Socrate."* (Università di Genova, Facoltà di lettere. Pubblicazione dell'Istituto di filologia classica, XIV.) Genoa: Cuneo, 1959.

LUCCIONI, JEAN. *Xénophon et le Socratisme.* (Publications de la faculté des lettres d'Alger, XXV.) Paris: Presses Universitaires, 1953.

MAGALHAES-VILHENA, V. DE. *Le Problème de Socrate*. Paris: Presses Universitaires, 1952.

———. *Socrate et la légende Platonicienne*. Paris: Presses Universitaires, 1952.

MAIER, HEINRICH. *Sokrates, sein Werk und seine geschichtliche Stellung*. Tübingen: J. C. B. Mohr, 1913.

SAUVAGE, MICHELINE. *Socrates and the Conscience of Man*. Translated by PATRICK HEPBOURNE-SCOTT New York: Harper & Brothers, 1960.

SPIEGELBERG, HERBERT, ed. *The Socratic Enigma*. "The Library of Liberal Arts," No. 192. New York: The Liberal Arts Press, Inc., 1964.

TAYLOR, A. E. *Socrates*. London: Peter Davies, 1951.

VOGEL, C. J. "The Present State of the Socratic Problem," *Phronesis*, I (1955/56), 26–35.

WINSPEAR, ALBAN D., and SILVERBERG, TOM. *Who Was Socrates?* New York: Russell & Russell, 1960. 2nd edition.

ZELLER, E. *Socrates and the Socratic Schools*. Translated by OSWALD J. REICHEL. London: Longmans, Green, 1868.

RECOLLECTIONS OF SOCRATES

or whatever gives responses, know what is beneficial for them, but they believe that the gods give signs through these mediaries; and this is what Socrates believed too.

4   Most people say that they are dissuaded or persuaded by birds or some such medium, but Socrates said what he knew to be the case: that a divinity gave him signs. Furthermore, he advised many of his companions to do or not to do something because the divinity had given him a sign beforehand; the people who heeded his advice were helped, while those who

5   did not, came to repent of it. Yet who would not agree that Socrates wanted to avoid appearing as a fool or impostor to his friends? He would have been considered both, had he made supposedly divine prophecies which then made a liar of him. Obviously, he would not have made prophecies if he had not believed them true. In matters of prophecy, who would respect someone other than a god? And if Socrates paid respect to gods, he must have thought that gods exist.

6   But to proceed, Socrates used to deal with his friends like this: when actions were necessary, he advised his friends how best to perform them. However, in regard to actions whose outcome was uncertain, he sent his friends to consult oracles

7   as to whether they should be done. "Men," he said, "need divination if they intend to manage home and state well. Men," he believed, "can comprehend and take lessons in things like carpentry, metalwork, farming, government, and the theory of these pursuits, as well as calculation, estate man-

8   agement, and strategy. However," he said, "the gods reserve for themselves the most important part of these activities, and this part man cannot foresee at all. The man who plants a field well does not know who will reap its fruits, and the man who builds a fine house does not know who will live in it. The general does not know if it will be profitable to conduct a campaign, and the politician does not know if it will be profitable to lead his state. The man who marries a beautiful bride in order to be happy does not know whether she will bring him sorrow. The man who has powerful connections in the state does not know whether he will be exiled from the

state through them. Men who consider that such questions *9*
have nothing to do with divinity, but are rather in the realm
of human reason, are mad," said Socrates. "They are mad,
also, if they consult oracles on questions about which the
gods permit men to make judgments. Suppose, for example,
a man asks whom he should get to drive his chariot, an experienced charioteer or an inexperienced man. Whom should
he hire to pilot a ship, a man who knows navigation or someone who does not? Men are mad if they consult oracles on
questions which they can answer if only they count, measure,
or weigh." Socrates believed that men who asked the gods
such questions were committing lawless acts. "What the gods
permit us to learn to do," he said, "we must learn by ourselves. But what is hidden from man we must try to learn
from the gods by divination, for the gods give signs to the
men to whom they are propitious."

Socrates was always out in the public eye. Early in the *10*
morning he went to promenades and the gymnasiums. When
the agora was crowded, he appeared there. During the rest of
the day, he always went where he might expect to meet the
most people. Most of the time he was talking, and anyone who
pleased could listen. No one ever saw or heard Socrates say *11*
or do anything irreverent or unholy. He did not hold discussions on the nature of the universe as most of the others did,
and he did not speculate as to what the "cosmos," as the
sophists call it, was like, or by what laws each part of the
heavens came into being. Furthermore, he declared that people who even thought about such matters were foolish. He *12*
would first ask them whether they entered upon investigation
of these problems because they thought they knew enough
about human affairs, or whether they thought that they were
doing their duty by dismissing human affairs and speculating
on divine concerns.

He was amazed that they did not realize such questions are *13*
impossible for men to answer, since those who most pride
themselves on discussing these questions do not agree with
each other, but behave toward one another like madmen.

14   "Some of these madmen do not fear what is fearful, and
others are afraid of things that are not to be feared. Some
feel no shame in saying or doing anything even in public;
others think that they ought not to go out among men. Some
do not revere shrines, altars, or anything divine; some revere
stones, chance bits of wood, and beasts. Of the men who concern themselves with the nature of the universe, some think
that it is only one being; [3] others that it is an infinite plural-
ity; [4] some that it is in constant flux,[5] others that it is never
moved.[6] Some say, 'Everything comes into being and is destroyed'; some, 'Nothing ever comes into being or is destroyed.'"

15   These were not the only questions that Socrates raised about
the theorists. "Like the men who learn human knowledge and
believe that they will apply their knowledge for their own
advantage or for whomever they choose, so men who study
divine questions think that when they know the laws by which
everything comes into being, they will, when they choose,
create winds, water, seasons, and anything else like these that
they may need. Or have they no hope for any such thing, but
find it enough simply to know how each of these phenomena
16   occurs?" This is what Socrates had to say to the men who dealt
with these questions. As for himself, he was always discussing
human problems and examining questions like, "What is reverence?" "What is irreverence?" "What is good? or evil? or jus-
tive? or injustice?" "What is temperance? madness? courage?
cowardice?" "What is a state? a politician?" "What is a government?" "What is a ruler?"—and the rest of these questions.
Men who know the answers to questions like these, he thought,
are truly noble, while the men who do not know deserve to
be called slaves.

17   We should not be amazed that the jurors erred in their
judgment about Socrates on those subjects about which his

3 E.g., Xenophanes.
4 E.g., Leucippus.
5 E.g., Heraclitus.
6 E.g., Zeno.

ingly strong when he faced cold, heat, and every imaginable hardship. Furthermore, he had so schooled himself to moderate needs that he had quite enough even when he possessed

2   very little. How could such a man make others irreverent, unlawful, gluttonous, lustful, or weak in the face of hardship? Socrates kept many men from these vices by making them desire virtue, and offering them the hope that, if only they dis-

3   ciplined themselves, they would become truly noble men. Yet he never promised to teach this; rather, because he clearly was truly noble, he made his companions hope to become like him

4   by imitating him. Moreover, Socrates did not neglect his body, nor did he praise those who did so. On the one hand, he disapproved of overexertion after overeating, and on the other hand, he approved of exercising as much as the soul enjoyed. He claimed that the habit of hard exercise was quite healthy

5   and did not impede the care of the soul. He was not at all effeminate or pretentious, in his clothing, his shoes, or any other fashion. He did not arouse love of money in his companions, because he kept them from other kinds of desire and,

6   when they desired him, he did not ask for money. He believed that he was safeguarding his freedom when he avoided accepting money, and he denounced as slaves the men who accepted pay for their conversation, since they were forced to

7   talk with anyone from whom they received pay. He was continually amazed that anybody who professed to teach virtue asked for money instead of considering the opportunity of winning a good friend the highest pay possible. How could he fear that a man who had become truly noble would not have the deepest gratitude for the teacher who had given him the

8   greatest possible benefit! Socrates never professed to teach virtue. He believed that his companions who accepted what he approved would be good friends to him, and to each other, all of their lives. How could a man like this ever corrupt the young? Unless the cultivation of virtue corrupts!

9   "But, by Zeus!" said the prosecutor.[1] "He made his com-

---

[1] The man referred to throughout the rest of chapter 2 as *the prosecutor* (12, 26, 49, 51, 56, 58) is probably Polycrates. See Introduction, pp. xiv–xv.

panions despise the established laws by saying that it was foolish for the archons of the state to be chosen by lot and that
no one would be willing to choose a pilot, builder, or flutist
by lot—yet mistakes in such tasks cause much less harm than
mistakes in ruling the state. Such arguments made the young
despise the established constitution and made them violent."
I, however, think that those who seek prudence and believe 10
they are able to teach citizens what is to the advantage of the
state are the last people to become violent. Such men know
that enmities and dangers accompany violence, while persuasion, without involving any risk, produces the same results,
and friendship in the bargain. Being coerced, like being
robbed, makes men feel hatred, but yielding to persuasion, like
doing favors, makes men feel friendship. Force is characteristic
not of men who seek prudence, but of men who wield power
without reasoning. But the fact is that the man who dares to 11
use force needs many allies, while the man who is able to
persuade needs none because he realizes that he can gain his
point singlehanded. Such men have no occasion to kill, for
who would wish to take a life rather than have a living follower? "But," said the prosecutor, "Critias and Alcibiades 12
were associates of Socrates, and they wrought the greatest harm
to the state. Critias was the most rapacious and violent of all
in the oligarchy, while Alcibiades was the most intemperate
and insolent of all the democracy." I shall not defend these 13
two, if they did any evil to the state. I shall explain, however,
how it happened that they became companions of Socrates.
These two men were by nature the most ambitious of all 14
Athenians. They wished to control everything and to be the
most famous. They knew that Socrates was living a completely
independent life on the scantiest means, that he was extremely
self-controlled in all pleasures, and that in his discussions he
dealt as he wished with all who disputed with him. These two 15
men saw this and were like what I have described. Now, is
there anyone who would claim that the two of them sought
out Socrates' company because they desired Socrates' way of
life or his temperance? Isn't it rather that they thought that

if they associated with him, they would become very proficient
16   in speech and action? For my part, I believe that if a god had
given them a choice of death or of living all their lives as they
saw Socrates live, they would have preferred to die. Their actions revealed what they were, for as soon as they believed
themselves to be superior to their fellow men, they immediately left Socrates and entered politics—the very end for which
they had sought him out.

17   Someone may answer what I have said as follows: "Before Socrates taught his companions politics, he should have
taught them temperance." I do not deny this. I note, however,
that all teachers show their students how they themselves do
what they teach, and then use reasoning to persuade their students to do it. I know as well that Socrates appeared to his
companions to be truly noble, and that he argued best on the
18   subject of virtue and other similar human concerns. I know
too that even Critias and Alcibiades were temperate as long as
they were with Socrates, not because they were afraid of being
penalized or beaten by Socrates, but because, at that time,
they thought that this was the best conduct.

19   Many who pretend to be philosophers will say, perhaps,
that a just man can never become unjust or a temperate man
insolent, or that no one can ever become ignorant of the
knowledge that he has learned. For my part, I do not share
this opinion. This is the analogy that I see: just as men who
fail to train their bodies cannot perform the body's functions,
so men who fail to train the soul cannot perform the soul's
functions, for they cannot do what they ought to do or avoid
20   what they ought not to do. This is the reason that fathers try
to keep their sons, even if they are already temperate, away
from bad company. The society of good men is training in virtue, but the society of evil men is the ruin of virtue. One of
the poets [2] bears witness to this when he says, "You learn
what is noble from the noble. If you mingle with evil men,
you will destroy the mind you had." Another poet [3] says, "He

[2] Theognis.
[3] The poet is unknown.

is a good man, though he is sometimes evil and sometimes noble." I myself can testify to this, for I see that, just as men forget poetry which they do not repeat, so they forget the words of a teacher, if they neglect them. When a man forgets words of advice, he forgets the very things that cause the soul, upon hearing them, to desire temperance; and when he forgets this, it is not surprising that he forgets temperance as well. I see, also, that those who are led to drunkenness and those who become involved in love affairs lose the power to do what they should do and to avoid what they should not do. Many are able to be careful about money until they fall in love. When they fall in love, they can no longer be careful. After they have spent their money lavishly, they do not refrain from making the kind of profits which they had previously considered disgraceful. How, then, is it impossible for the man who once was temperate to be intemperate, and for the man who once was able to act justly to be unable to do so any longer? It seems to me that good and noble things, especially temperance, are acquired by practice. For pleasures have been planted in the same body as the soul; and they beg the soul not to be temperate, but to make haste to gratify themselves and the body.

As long as Critias and Alcibiades were companions of Socrates, they were able, with him as an ally, to master their evil desires. The two, however, left Socrates. Critias fled to Thessaly [4] and there associated with men who lived by lawlessness rather than by justice. Alcibiades, on the other hand, was pursued by many respected women [5] because of his beauty; he was courted by many influential men because of his power in Athens and among Athens' allies; he was honored by the people, and easily won positions of leadership. [6] Like athletes

[4] When Critias fled in exile from Athens, he went to Thessaly, proverbial for its lawlessness. After his return to Athens in 404, he became a leading member of the oligarchy and one of the Thirty Tyrants. See note 7, p. 13 and Introduction, pp. xv, xviii.

[5] For example, his affair with the wife of the King of Sparta during his exile from Athens was notorious.

[6] Alcibiades was general in 415 B.C. and again in 408 B.C.

who win athletic contests easily, and therefore neglect their
25   training, Alcibiades neglected himself. This is what happened
to the two men, so that they became swollen with family pride,
elated with wealth, inflated with power, and spoiled by popular favor. After they had been corrupted by all this, and had
been away from Socrates for a long time, is it any wonder that
they became arrogant?

26   If these two played false notes, then, does the prosecutor
blame Socrates for it? When they were young and most likely
to be ignorant and intemperate, Socrates made them temperate. Doesn't the prosecutor think that Socrates deserves praise
27   for this? No one judges other cases this way. What flute player,
citharist, or some other kind of teacher, is to be blamed, if
after he has made his pupils proficient, they go to someone
else and make a worse showing? If a child is temperate when
he spends his time with one teacher but becomes evil when
later he associates with another, does the father blame the
first teacher? On the contrary, the worse the son appears because of the second teacher, the more the father praises the
first. As long as fathers live temperately when they are with
their sons, they aren't blamed when their sons make mistakes.
28   We should judge Socrates in the same way. If he himself usually did evil, it would be reasonable to consider him wicked.
If he lived temperately, then how could he justly be blamed
29   for evil that was not in him? But if Socrates, while doing
nothing wicked himself, had kept on praising Critias and
Alcibiades when he saw them doing evil, it would be quite
just to censure him. When, however, he saw that Critias loved
Euthydemus and was trying to make use of him as men do
who enjoy the body in sexual pleasure, he tried to dissuade
Critias by saying that it was ignoble and unfitting for a truly
noble man to ask his beloved—the very man from whom he
wanted esteem—to give what is not good to give, and like a
pauper to beg and importune him for it.

30   But Critias did not listen to this advice and he was not dissuaded. So they tell that in front of many others, including
Euthydemus, Socrates said that he thought Critias behaved

like a pig, desiring to rub himself against Euthydemus as pigs
do against stones. As a result of this Critias hated Socrates, *31*
and when he and Charicles, as members of the Thirty,[7] became
lawmakers, he remembered his grudge against Socrates, and
among the laws he enacted was one that forbade the teaching
of the art of argument. He insulted Socrates this way because
he had no other way of attacking him, and he slandered Socrates before the people by imputing to him the practice for
which the people usually blamed the philosophers. I, for my
part, never heard Socrates teach the art of argument and I
never met anyone else who claims to have heard Socrates do
this. The truth came out. For when the Thirty put many citi- *32*
zens to death—and not just unimportant ones either—and
urged many others to commit injustices, Socrates said somewhere that he would be amazed if a herdsman of cattle who
decreased the herd and made it worse would not admit that he
was a bad cowherd. Yet it was even more amazing if a leader
of the state who decreased the number of citizens and made
them worse did not feel ashamed and consider himself a bad
chief of state. When they heard this, Critias and Charicles *33*
summoned Socrates, showed him the law, and warned him not
to hold discussions with the young. Socrates asked the two if
he might ask questions about anything he did not understand
in the law. The two said yes. "Then," he said, "I am prepared *34*
to obey the laws. But so that I won't make a mistake and tres-
pass them through ignorance, I want a clear explanation from
you whether you think the art of argument deals with sound
or with unsound reasoning, when you order me to avoid it. If
with sound reasoning, obviously one must abstain from sound
reasoning. If with unsound reasoning, obviously one must try
to reason soundly."

Charicles was enraged at him and replied, "Since, Socrates, *35*
you are ignorant, we will make our commands easier to understand. You must not hold discussions with the young."

[7] The Thirty Tyrants comprised a committee from the oligarchical
party in Athens which was set up under Spartan influence after Sparta
defeated Athens. Their rule (404–403 B.C.) was a reign of terror. See Introduction, pp. xv, xviii.

Socrates said, "So that there may be no doubt, please define for me at what age I must consider men young."

"As long as they are not permitted to be in the Senate because they are not yet wise. Do not speak with men under thirty," replied Charicles.

36 "If I am buying something," he said, "and if a man under thirty is selling it, may I not even ask how much it costs?"

"You may ask such things," said Charicles, "but, Socrates, you usually ask most of your questions when you know the answers. These you are not to ask."

"Can't I even reply if a young man asks me, for example, if I know where the house of Charicles is or where Critias is?"

"Yes, such things are permitted," said Charicles.

37 "But you must avoid asking," said Critias, "about cobblers, builders, and metalworkers, for I think that they have already been worn out and exhausted by you."

"Then," said Socrates, "I must not talk even of the things of which these are illustrations—justice, holiness, and other similar subjects?"

"Right, by Zeus," said Charicles, "and you must not speak of cowherds. Be careful lest you cause a decrease in the number of cattle."

38 So it became clear that they had heard of the discussion about the cattle and were enraged at Socrates. The nature of the association and relationship between Critias and Socrates has now been described.

39 I would say, furthermore, that no one learns from a teacher whom he dislikes. Critias and Alcibiades spoke with Socrates, during the time when they held discourse with him, not because they liked him, but because right from the start they were eager to control the state. While they were yet companions of Socrates, they tried to hold discussions only with those who were most active in politics.

40 It is said that before he was twenty years old, when his guardian was Pericles, leader of the state, Alcibiades held the following discussion with Pericles about law:

41 "Tell me, Pericles, could you explain to me what law is?"

"Of course," said Pericles.

"Then, by the gods, tell me," said Alcibiades. "When I hear men praised because they are law-abiding, I realize that a man who does not know what the law is would not earn this praise justly."

"You do not desire anything difficult, Alcibiades, when you *42* want to know what law is. All those are laws which the majority, after assembling and debating, enacts as to what should and should not be done."

"Which do they consider should be done? Good or evil?"

"By Zeus, my boy, good, of course! And they consider that evil should not be done."

"Suppose that instead of the majority, a few, as for example *43* in the case of an oligarchy, hold an assembly and enact what should be done. What is this called?"

"Everything the government in power in a state resolves and enacts about what should be done is called law," answered Pericles.

"If a tyrant holding power in a state enacts measures about what the citizens must do, are these called laws?" asked Alcibiades.

"Yes. All that the tyrant in power enacts is also called law."

"But what, Pericles, are force and lawlessness? Don't they *44* occur when a stronger person, instead of using persuasion, forces a weaker person to do what he decrees?"

"I think so," said Pericles.

"Then isn't it lawlessness if a tyrant does not use persuasion, but instead enacts measures and forces the citizens to carry them out?"

"Yes," said Pericles. "I retract my statement that every measure which a tyrant proposes without using persuasion is law."

"Would we, or would we not, call it force when a few in *45* power enact measures for the people without using persuasion?"

"I think," said Pericles, "that everything which someone, without using persuasion, forces another to do, whether by decree or not, is force, not law."

"Then isn't it force rather than law if the majority, prevailing over those who have money, make proposals and do not use persuasion?"

46   "Quite, Alcibiades! said Pericles, "and when we were your age, we too were very clever in such discussions. We studied and devised subtleties just as you are doing now, I think."

"I wish," said Alcibiades, "that I had been your companion, Pericles, when you excelled yourself in debate."

47   Therefore, just as soon as Alcibiades and Critias thought themselves superior to the politicians in power, they stopped associating with Socrates, for they did not like him for any other reason; and whenever they went to him, they resented being reproved for the wrong they did. They began to run the affairs of state, the purpose for which they had gone to Soc-

48 rates. In contrast to Alcibiades and Critias was Crito, Socrates' associate; also Chaerephon, Chaerecrates, Hermogenes, Simmias, Cebes, Phaedondas, and others as well who associated with Socrates—not so as to become public or forensic orators, but to become truly noble men who could manage their homes and slaves capably, as well as their families, friends, state, and fellow citizens. No one of these, either when young or old, ever did evil or incurred reproach.

49   "But," said the prosecutor, "Socrates taught his companions to abuse their parents by persuading them that he made them wiser than their parents and by claiming that according to the law it was possible for a son, if he proved his father insane, to imprison even his own father. As an argument for this, he said that is was right for the more ignorant man to be kept

50 in bondage by a wiser man." But Socrates meant this: that the man who puts someone in prison for ignorance could in his turn be imprisoned quite justly by those who know what he does not know. It was for this reason that he often used to ask, "What is the difference between ignorance and madness?" He believed that keeping madmen in bondage was advantageous to the madmen as well as to their friends, and that it was just for the men who did not know what they should know to learn from the men who knew.

51   "Socrates," said the prosecutor, "caused disrespect in his

associates, not only toward parents but also toward the rest of their relatives. He did this by saying that it is not relatives who are of use to the sick, or to the accused, but doctors and lawyers." The prosecutor also said that Socrates claimed it was useless to be well disposed to friends unless they could be of some service; also that Socrates claimed that the only men worthy of honor were those who knew their duty and could explain what they knew. Socrates, he said, also made the youth think that other men were of no account in comparison with himself, for he persuaded them that he was the wisest man and the most competent in making others wise. 52

53

I know that he used to say these things about parents, relatives, and friends; and in addition to this he even used to say that when the soul, the only place where prudence resides, left the body, men carry out and get rid of the body as quickly as possible, even that of the closest relative. Socrates used to point out that every man alive, if he does not do so himself, allows others to remove useless parts of his body, even though the body is what a man loves most of all. Either they themselves cut and burn off nails, hair, and calluses, or they allow doctors to do so, despite the pain and suffering involved. Men think they should even give thanks and money for this! They spit saliva from their mouths as far away as possible, because it is of no use to them inside and could do much harm. When Socrates said this, he was not teaching that we should bury our fathers alive or cut ourselves up! He was simply illustrating that senselessness is not worthy of esteem and was urging men to take the trouble to be as prudent and as useful as possible. If a man wants esteem from his father or brother or someone else, he should not neglect them and rely on the fact that they are close relatives. He should instead try to be useful to those from whom he desires esteem. 54

55

The prosecutor said that he chose the most wicked passages from the most famous poets, and used their authority to teach his followers to be evil and tyrannical. For example, the line from Hesiod: [8] "Work is not at all blameworthy, but idleness 56

8 *Works and Days* 311.

is." They said that Socrates explained this to mean that the poet bids us not to refrain from any work whether unjust or evil, but to do even unjust and evil works for gain. When Socrates agreed that a worker was both useful and good and that the idle man was harmful and evil, and that to work was good while to be idle was evil, he meant that those who do good are working and are good workers; those who play dice or engage in other wicked and profitless pursuits, on the other hand, he denounced as idle. With this interpretation, the passage, "Work is not at all blameworthy, but idleness is," is right. The prosecutor said that Socrates often quoted Odysseus: [9]

> When he met a kind or distinguished man, he stood beside him and addressed him with kindly words: "Noble sir, you do not seem to be so base as to be afraid. Sit down and make other people take their places." . . . But when he saw a man of the people and found him shouting in fear, he brandished his scepter and spoke to him: "Noble sir, stand firm, hear the words of those who are better than you. You are unwarlike and without strength, worthless both on the battlefield and in the Assembly."

The prosecutor claimed that Socrates interpreted this to mean that the poet praised the beating of the common people and of the humble. Socrates did not mean this. If he had, he would have thought that he himself should be beaten. He meant, rather, that men who, in time of need, were useful in neither word nor deed to the army, the state, or the people, especially if they added insolence to weakness, must be restrained in every way, even if they happened to be rich. Socrates was clearly quite the opposite of such men. He was a man of the people; he liked his fellow men. Although he had many devoted followers from Athens and elsewhere, he never took pay from anyone for his company, but to all alike he gave unstintingly of whatever he had. Some even took a small amount from him free and sold it to others at great price; unlike Socrates, these were not men of the people, and they refused to

[9] Homer, *Iliad* II. 188–91, 198–202.

hold discussions with people who did not have money. In his 61
dealings with all the rest of mankind, Socrates was much more
of an ornament to his state than Lichas was to Sparta. Yet
Lichas' fame became proverbial. Lichas entertained foreigners
who had come to Sparta to see the festival of Gymnopaediae.[10]
Socrates, on the other hand, all through his life, gave the highest services, at his own expense, to all who wished: he made
his associates better, and then he sent them away.

Since Socrates was like this, I think he deserved honor, not 62
death, from his state. And anyone who considers the case
from a legal standpoint will find this out. For under our laws,
it is thieves, robbers, pickpockets, housebreakers, kidnapers,
or temple-robbers who are subject to the penalty of death.
Socrates was further from being any of these than any man
known. He never brought war, revolution, treason, or any evil 63
upon the state. In private life, he never deprived any man of
anything good, he never involved anyone in evil, and he was
never charged with any of the evils we have mentioned. How 64
could he be guilty of the charges? Instead of "not paying respect to the gods," as the indictment read, he served the gods
more than men usually do; instead of "corrupting the young,"
as the prosecutor kept charging, he openly kept his associates
away from evil when they desired to do evil, and he encouraged them to pursue the highest and noblest virtue by which
states and homes prosper. In view of his conduct, how could
he not deserve honor from his state?

Chapter 3: Socrates' Teachings on Religion and on Self-control

Inasmuch as Socrates was, I believe, useful to his associ- 1
ates, both through his actions in which he revealed what he
was like and through the discussions he held, I shall now write

[10] The Gymnopaediae was a Spartan festival in honor of Apollo, Artemis, and Latona commemorating a Spartan victory over the Argives. Its
name derived from the choruses of nude men and boys which danced.
Lichas fed foreign visitors to the festival at his own expense.

what I recollect of these words and deeds. Toward the gods, he clearly acted and spoke in accordance with the responses of the Pythian priestess [1] to questions about how to act regarding sacrifices, ancestor-worship, or anything else like that. For the Pythian priestess ordains that men act reverently if they follow the law of the state. Socrates himself followed this conduct and encouraged others to do so, and he thought that men who did otherwise were presumptuous and foolish. He

2 used to pray to the gods simply for "good things" because the gods know best what kinds of things are good. When men pray for gold, silver, sovereignty, or anything else of this sort, it is just like praying about dice, a battle, or something else

3 of which the outcome is quite uncertain. Though he made but humble sacrifices from his humble means, he did not consider himself inferior to the men who sacrificed frequently and magnificently from ample and magnificent means. "It would not be fair of the gods," he said, "if they were more pleased by large sacrifices than by small ones. If that were the case, the sacrifices of the wicked would often be more delightful to them than the sacrifices of the righteous. Life would not be worthwhile for men if the gifts of the wicked were more pleasing to the gods than the gifts of the righteous." The gods, he believed, rejoiced the most at reverence coming from the most pious men. He approved this saying: "Do sacrifice to the immortal gods according to your power," [2] and he would add that to "do according to your power" was good advice in our behavior toward friends and strangers and in

4 our general conduct. If ever he thought he had received a sign from the gods, nothing could persuade him to go against the divine sign. It would have been easier to persuade him to accept the guidance of a blind man who did not know his way instead of looking for the way himself, than to persuade him to act contrary to the divine sign. He accused of stupidity the others who did anything contrary to signs from the gods because they were eager to avoid ill fame among men. He him-

---

[1] The Pythian priestess gave Apollo's oracles at Delphi.
[2] Hesiod, *Works and Days* 336.

self considered all human things despicable compared to counsel from the gods.

The mode of life by which he educated his soul and body   *5*
was such that anyone who followed it could live confidently
and securely without failing to have enough to spend, unless
of course something superhuman intervened. He was so frugal that no one could imagine how to work so little as not
to earn enough for Socrates' needs. He consumed as much
food as he could eat with pleasure, and was so ready for his
food that his appetite for food was its spice. He liked any
drink at all because he did not drink unless he was thirsty.
Whenever he accepted an invitation to come to dinner, he   *6*
very easily kept from eating and drinking too much—very
difficult for most people! He advised men who could not do
this to avoid food that stimulated their appetites and thirst
when they were not hungry or thirsty. "These appetizers only
ruin the stomach, the head, and the soul," he said. Laugh-   *7*
ingly he added that he thought that Circe turned men into
pigs by feeding them many such foods, and that Odysseus
avoided becoming a pig because of Hermes' advice and his own
self-control, and because he avoided eating these foods in ex-
cess.[3] This is what Socrates said, half in jest and half in earn-   *8*
est, about eating and drinking.

He advised men to keep resolutely away from sexual intercourse with beautiful boys, for once a man has had such experiences it is not easy for him to be temperate. One time
Socrates heard that Critobulus, the son of Crito, had kissed
Alcibiades' son, who was a very beautiful boy; he asked Xenophon, right in the presence of Critobulus, "Xenophon, did   *9*
you once think that Critobulus was a temperate, cautious,
and sensible man, neither rash, nor senseless, nor adventurous?"

"Of course," said Xenophon.

"From now on, then, consider him a man who is hotheaded
and who would dare anything. He would do somersaults in
the midst of knives and leap into fire!"

[3] Socrates alludes to the story of the witch Circe, Homer, *Odyssey* X.
135 ff.

10   "What have you seen him do that makes you condemn him like this?"

Socrates answered, "Didn't he dare to kiss Alcibiades' son, who is so very good-looking and beautiful?"

"But if this is the perilous deed," said Xenophon, "I myself would run the risk, I think!"

11   "Wretch," replied Socrates, "what do you think will happen to you if you kiss a handsome boy? Won't you immediately become a slave, lose your freedom, spend lots of money on harmful pleasures, have very little leisure to cultivate what is truly noble, and be forced to pursue what only a madman would pursue?"

12   "By Heracles!" said Xenophon. "What dread power you impute to a kiss!"

"Does this too amaze you?" said Socrates. "Don't you know that spiders that are even smaller than hemiobols can kill men with pain and drive them out of their wits with only a tiny bite?"

"Yes, by Zeus!" said Xenophon. "For spiders inject something with their sting."

13   "Fool!" said Socrates. "Simply because you cannot see it, do you think that handsome men do not inject something when they kiss? Don't you realize that this wild animal called the fair and handsome boy is much more dangerous than a spider? Spiders must touch you while this creature—without even touching anyone, but simply by his looks—injects a poison from a distance that drives men mad. Perhaps this is the reason that love is called an archer: because he is beautiful and can wound even from a distance. I advise you, Xenophon, to flee headlong when you see a fair boy. And Critobulus, I advise you to spend a year abroad. You could hardly recover your health, in even that much time!"

14   He thought, then, that men who were not reliable in the face of their passions ought to have sexual intercourse only with such as the soul would not accept were it not that the body needed them, such as would not make trouble when the body did not need them. He had so trained himself that it was clearly easier for him to keep away from the fairest and

handsomest than it is for others to keep away from the ugli-
est and most repulsive.

In eating, drinking, and sexual pleasures, he had trained   *15*
himself as I have described, and he considered that he had
about as much pleasure as the men who indulge themselves
frequently, and certainly much less pain than they.

Chapter 4: Conversations with Aristodemus on Religion

If any think, as some write and say on the basis of mere   *1*
conjecture, that Socrates was extremely influential in exhort-
ing men to virtue yet powerless to lead them to it, they should
examine not only the punishment he dealt out in cross-ex-
amining the men who thought they knew everything, but also
the conversations in which he passed the time of day with
his friends. Then let them judge whether he was capable of
making his companions better. I shall first tell what I once   *2*
heard him say about divinity, in the course of a discussion
with Aristodemus "the Small," as he was nicknamed. When
Socrates discovered that Aristodemus did not sacrifice to the
gods or consult oracles, but even mocked such things, he said,
"Tell me, Aristodemus, aren't there any men whom you admire for their wisdom?"

"Yes, there are."

"Who? Tell me their names," said Socrates.

"In epic poetry, I admire Homer most of all; in dithyramb,   *3*
Melanippides; in tragedy, Sophocles. In sculpture, Polyclitus;
in painting, Zeuxis."

"Who do you think deserves more admiration? Those who   *4*
create images without sense or power to move, or those who
create living beings able to think and act?"

"By Zeus, of course those who create living beings, provided
they come into being through design, not by some chance."

"Suppose there are things which give no hint as to the purpose of their existence, and also things which clearly serve

a useful purpose. Which do you judge to be works of chance and which works of design?"

"Works that serve a useful end must be works of design."

5   "Don't you think that, from the very first, the creator of men endowed us with senses for a useful purpose? With eyes to see visible objects, and ears to hear sounds? What use would odors be to us if we had no nose? Would we taste sweet, bitter, and all the delights of the palate if our tongue had not

6   been made to taste them? Besides, don't you think that other things, too, are likely to be the result of forethought? The sense of sight is weak, for example, and therefore the eyes are given eyelids which, like doors, open wide when we have to use our eyes and close when we sleep. Eyelashes grow, like screens, so that the wind does not hurt our eyes. Above the eyes, eyebrows project like cornices to prevent harm from the sweat of the brow. There is also the fact that ears receive all sounds, but never are clogged up. The front teeth in all living beings are designed to cut; the molars to receive food from the incisors and to grind it. The mouth, through which enter the things that living beings desire, was placed near the eyes and nose. Since excrements are unpleasant, the ducts that get rid of them are as far as possible from the sense organs. When these have been made with so much foresight, are you at a loss to say whether they are the works of chance or of design?"

7   "No, by Zeus!" replied Aristodemus. "When I look at it that way, they do appear to be the works of a wise and loving creator."

"What of the desire to beget children, the mother's desire to raise her children, the children's longing to live, and the great fear of death?"

"To be sure, they seem to be the contrivances of someone who planned for living creatures to exist."

"Do you think that you have any prudence?" asked Socrates.

8   "Ask and I shall reply!" [1]

[1] It is not certain whether Aristodemus' reply means a modest "Yes," or "Judge for yourself from my answers," or "Continue asking, and I shall answer later."

"Do you think that prudence exists nowhere else? Even though you know that you have in your body only a tiny part of the earth that exists in great quantity, and only a drop of all the abundant waters that exist, and that your body is compounded of just a small part of each of the other elements that are, surely, abundant—do you think that you somehow, by luck, snatched up the only bit of mind that, it seems, exists nowhere else? That these masses, huge and infinite in number, are well arranged, as you suppose, through some absurdity?"

"Yes, by Zeus!" replied Aristodemus. "For I do not see the *9* masters as I see the men who make things here on earth."

"Nor do you see your soul, which is master of your body! By your reasoning, then, you could say that nothing you do is by design, but everything is by chance."

Aristodemus said, "Socrates, I don't really despise deity; *10* I simply think that it is too great to need my services."

Socrates replied, "Surely the greater the power that condescends to serve you, the more honor it deserves."

"You must know," he said, "that if I thought the gods *11* cared at all about men, I would not neglect them."

"Then you don't think that they care? First of all, they made man the only one of living creatures to stand erect, and this upright position makes it possible for him to see farther in front of him, to look more easily above him, and to suffer less harm; they also gave him sight, hearing, and a mouth. Secondly, while to creatures who walk on all fours the gods gave feet, which are good only for locomotion, they gave to man hands, which do most of the things that make us happier than beasts."

While it is true that all animals have a tongue, the gods *12* made only the tongue of man able, by touching the different parts of the mouth, to create sounds, and to communicate to other people what we wish. They limited the season of the year in which they gave other animals the pleasures of sexual intercourse, but to us they granted these continuously until old age.

13   Not only was the god pleased to take care of the body, but what is most important, he has planted in man the soul which is man's most powerful part. What other creature possesses a soul that, first of all, perceives the existence of the gods, who have established the greatest and most wonderful order? What species, except man, worships gods? What soul is more capable than the human soul in taking precautions against hunger, thirst, heat, and cold, or in preventing diseases, exercising bodily strength, working hard for knowledge; what species

14 is better able to remember what it hears, sees, or learns? Don't you see that in comparison with other living creatures, men live like gods and are naturally superior in body and soul? Even if he had the body of an ox and the mind of a man, a man could not do what he wanted. If he had hands and not reason, he still would have no advantage. Even though you have received both hands and reason, gifts of the greatest worth, do you think that the gods have no concern for you? What must they do before you will believe that they take care of you?

15   "When, as you say they do, they send advisers as to what we should and should not do," replied Aristodemus.

Socrates continued, "But when they give answers to the Athenians who ask something through divination, don't you think that they are answering them, or when they send omens to warn the Greeks, or all men? Are you the only one they

16 have singled out and selected for neglect? Do you think that the gods would plant in men the belief in their power to do good and evil, unless they were able to do so? Do you think that men would never have perceived the deception? Don't you see that the oldest and wisest of human institutions, city-states and nations, are the most reverent toward the gods, and that the most prudent periods of man's life are the most con-

17 cerned with gods? My dear sir," Socrates continued, "you should understand that your mind within deals with your body as it wants. You therefore should realize that universal thought [tēn en tōi panti phronēsin] disposes of everything as it pleases. Do not think that your eye can see many miles and

the god's eye cannot see the universe all at once, or that your soul can be concerned with things here, and in Egypt and Sicily as well, while the god's mind [*tēn tou theou phronēsin*] is unable to take care of the universe all at once. Just as by *18* serving men you discover who is willing to serve you in return, and by doing a favor who will return the favor, and by taking advice you discover who is prudent—so you should make trial of the gods by serving them to see if they want to counsel you about matters hidden to men. You will know that the divine is so great and of such a nature that it sees and hears everything at once, is present everywhere, and is concerned with everything."

I thought that Socrates, by saying things like this, kept his *19* companions from doing unholy, unjust, or evil acts, not only when they could be seen by men, but even in a desert; for they would believe that nothing they might do would escape the notice of the gods.

Chapter 5: A Discourse on Self-control

Since, moreover, self-control also is a truly noble possession *1* for a man, let us see whether Socrates led men to it by talking as follows:

"Gentlemen, suppose we are at war and should want to select a man to save us and deliver us from the enemy. Should we choose a man who, we perceive, gives in to hunger, wine, sexual desires, fatigue, and sleep? How should we ever imagine that a man like this might save us and conquer the enemy? As we near the end of our life, if we want someone whom we *2* can trust to educate our sons, protect our daughters, and keep our property intact, should we think that a man who lacks self-control would be the most trustworthy in doing this? Should we entrust our cattle, our storehouses, or the management of work to an intemperate slave? Should we be willing to accept such a servant or steward, even as a free gift?

"And if we should not have an intemperate slave, why *3*

should the master not think it right to avoid intemperance? It isn't like the case of grasping men who defraud others of their possessions and seem to grow rich. The intemperate man does not harm other men and benefit himself. Instead, he injures other men and does even worse injury to himself—that is, if you admit that the greatest injury to him is not the destruction of his home, but that of his body and soul. In social dealings, who can like the sort of man who, you know, prefers your rich food and wine to your friends, and loves prostitutes more than your companions? Should not all men consider self-control the foundation of virtue, and train their souls first and foremost in this? What man without self-control can learn any good, or do any good worth mentioning? What slave to pleasure is not evil in both body and soul? I think, by Hera, that every free man should pray not to have such a slave, and that every man who is a slave to such pleasures should beseech the gods to give him good masters, since that is the only way for such a man to be saved."

This is what Socrates said about self-control, and his actions showed even more self-control than his words. He controlled not only the pleasures of the body, but also the pleasures that money can buy, because he believed that the man who takes money from the man who just happens to pass by is placing himself under a master and serving the most evil slavery of all.

Chapter 6: Conversations with Antiphon

I owe it to Socrates not to omit an argument which he had with the sophist Antiphon,[1] who once came to Socrates to lure Socrates' companions away. In their presence, he addressed Socrates as follows: "Socrates, I thought that philosophers should be very happy. But you seem to have derived quite the opposite from philosophy. At any rate, you live in a way that

[1] Nothing more is known of the sophist Antiphon than Xenophon describes, except Aristotle's statement that he was a contemporary and opponent of Socrates.

would drive a slave away, should his master provide him with a similar living. You eat and drink the poorest stuff. You not only wear a cheap coat, but you wear the same coat winter and summer. You are always barefoot and ill-clad. You don't ac- 3 cept money, which brings cheer as you earn it and makes life freer and easier when you possess it. If you make your com- panions imitate you as the teachers of other pursuits make their students imitate them, consider yourself a teacher of un- happiness."

Socrates replied, "Antiphon, you seem to assume that I am 4 living in so much distress that you would choose to die, I be- lieve, rather than live as I live. But let us look into what you think is so difficult about my life. Is it that men who make 5 money must do what they are hired for, while I, because I won't accept money, don't have to hold discussions with any- one unless I want to? And do you consider my diet poor be- cause I eat less healthful or less nourishing food than you, or because it is more difficult to find my foods than yours, since they are scarcer and more expensive? Do you think that the food you provide for yourself is more enjoyable than what I provide for myself? Don't you know that the man who most enjoys food has the least need of sauces, and the man who most enjoys drinking has the least desire for drinking when there are no drinks available? As for coats, you know that peo- 6 ple who change do so because of the heat and cold, and they wear shoes so as to keep their feet from being hurt. Now then, have you ever seen me stay inside because of the cold or, when it is hot, fight with someone for shade, or because of pain in my feet not walk where I want? Aren't you aware that even the 7 men who are naturally very weak in body become stronger and have more endurance, through training, than the strongest men who neglect their training? Don't you think that I, who am constantly training to be strong in the face of whatever befalls the body, can endure everything more easily than you, who are not in training? Do you think that there is any more effective 8 cause of not being a slave to the stomach, to sleep, or to lust, than to have other, more delightful pleasures which not only give enjoyment when used, but also offer hope of continual benefit? Don't you really know that the men who believe they are not successful in anything are unhappy, while the men who believe that they make progress in farming, shipping, or any other work they happen to do, are happy because they are successful? Do you think that there is as much pleasure from these sources as from the belief that you are becoming better and possess better friends? I, therefore, continue to believe this. If friends or state need help, who has more leisure to come to their aid? Someone who lives as I, or someone who lives what you call the "happy" way of life? Who can campaign with the army more easily, the man unable to live without luxuries or the man for whom whatever he can get is enough? Which man under siege will give in more quickly? The one who demands what is hard to find or the one who is satisfied with what is easy to get? Antiphon, you are like the people who think that happiness is luxurious and expensive. I, for my part, have always thought that to need nothing is divine and to have the fewest needs is the next thing to divine; that the divine is supreme and that to be next to the divine is to be next to the supreme."

On another occasion Antiphon said to Socrates in an argument, "Socrates, I consider you to be just, but not at all wise. You yourself, I think, realize this, since you don't exact payments for conversation with you. Yet if you thought that your coat or house or anything else you own were worth money, you would not give it away free or sell it for less than its value. Clearly, if you thought that you were of any value to your friends, you would exact payment for what you are worth. Therefore, you may be just, since you do not cheat from greed, but you are not wise; for the things you know are not worth anything at all."

Socrates replied, "Antiphon, with us, the belief is that our beauty and wisdom can be used for good or for evil. If someone sells his beauty for money to the one who wants it, they call him a fornicator. If a man becomes a friend to a lover who he knows is truly noble, we consider him temperate. It is the same in regard to wisdom: men are called 'sophists' if they sell wisdom for money to anyone who wants it. When, however, a man teaches a person who he knows is gifted all the good he can and makes him a friend, we consider that he is doing the duty of a truly noble citizen. I myself, Antiphon, *14* like anyone else who delights in a fine horse, bird, or dog, am even more delighted by good friends. If I have something to teach, I teach it and I introduce my associates to others from whom I believe they will get some benefit in their search for virtue. The treasures which the wise men of old have left in scrolls, we unroll and peruse together with our friends and we pick out any good we may discover. We think the gain is great if we become friends to one another." When I heard Socrates say this, I thought that he was happy, and that he led those who heard him toward true nobility.

Another time, Antiphon asked him how he thought he *15* made men into politicians when he himself took no part in politics, even granting he did have a knowledge of politics. "Antiphon," Socrates replied, "would I be engaging in politics more by taking part in them alone, or by taking care that as many men as possible are capable of engaging in politics?"

Chapter 7: On False Pretensions

Let us turn now to the next question: Was Socrates persuad- *1* ing his companions to pursue virtue when he dissuaded them from false pretensions? Socrates continually repeated that there was no better road to fame than that by which a man became really good in the field in which he wished to be considered good. This is the way he taught the truth of what he said. "Let us suppose," he said, "that someone who was a poor *2* flutist wished to be considered a good flutist. What should he do? Shouldn't he imitate the good flutists in the externals of his art? First of all, because they possess fine clothes and gather many followers around them, he also must do this. Then, because many praise the good flutist, he too must arrange for applause. Of course, he must never accept work, or else he will immediately be exposed as ridiculous, a bad flutist, and, what is more, an imposter. So while he goes to great expense and gains no profit at all, he gets a bad reputation as well. Of course his life will be troublesome, useless, and laughable. In the same way, if a man who is not a good general or navigator should wish to appear one, let us imagine what would happen to him. Isn't it true that if he wished to seem efficient in this, yet could not convince anyone, it would be painful; but that it would be even more disastrous if he convinced anyone that he was good? Clearly the man who does not know how to pilot a ship or to be a general, if placed in charge, would destroy those whom he least wanted to destroy and would emerge disgraced and shameful." In the same way, Socrates proved that it was useless for a man to try to seem wealthy, brave, or strong when he was not. "For duties beyond their abilities are assigned to these men," he said, "and when they are not able to perform them, since they seem to be capable, they find no mercy." He used to call a man a cheat if the man persuaded another to lend him money or supplies and then defrauded him. "But the biggest cheat of all," he said, "is the man who by deceit persuades his state that he is able to lead it and yet is not able to." I was of the opinion that by such arguments Socrates dissuaded his companions from false pretensions.

BOOK TWO

SOCRATIC CONVERSATIONS

Chapter 1: With Aristippus on Self-control

I thought that when Socrates held the conversation I am ¹ about to report, he was persuading his companions to practice self-control in their desire for food, drink, sex, and sleep, and in their endurance of cold, heat, and fatigue. When he became aware that one of his companions was intemperate in such matters, he said, "Aristippus, if you had to take into your charge and educate two young men so that the one would be fit to rule and the other would not seek for power at all, how would you educate each one? Would you consider the question by beginning with the fundamental problem, that of food?" Aristippus said, "I certainly think that food is the thing to begin with, for no one could exist without nourishment." Socrates said, "The desire for food, whenever the right time ² comes, naturally occurs in both."

"Yes, naturally."

"Which of these would you train to choose to do urgent business before satisfying his appetite?"

"The one being educated to rule, by Zeus!" said Aristippus, "so that the business of state might not be left undone during his term of office."

"When they want to have a drink," said Socrates, "should not the same one be given the power to endure thirst?"

"Of course."

"To whom should we give self-control in sleep, so that he ³ can go to sleep late and arise early, and even go without sleep if he must?"

"To the same one," replied Aristippus.

"And self-control over his sexual urges, so that nothing will prevent him from doing what must be done?"

"Again, the same one."

"To which should we give the power to do work willingly without shirking?"

"This, also, to the one being educated to rule."

"To whom is it more fitting to give the knowledge necessary for overcoming his opponents?"

"To the one being educated to rule, by Zeus! The other lessons are useless without the knowledge of that."

"Then," said Socrates, "you think that the boy educated this way is less likely than other creatures to be trapped by his opponents? Some of these, you know, are trapped by food— even some timid creatures who are nevertheless lured to the bait by their desire to eat and are captured. Others are ensnared by drink."

"Undoubtedly," replied Aristippus.

"Still other animals are ensnared by lust, like quails and partridges who, at the sound of the female call, are carried away by lust and the anticipation of sexual intercourse. They lose their power to calculate shrewdly, and fall into nets." Aristippus agreed with this as well. "Don't you think it a disgrace for men to suffer the same fate as the most senseless of beasts? Thus, adulterers enter the women's quarters even though they know that they are running the risk of suffering what the law threatens, or of being trapped, caught, and assaulted. Although such evils and disgrace lie in store for adulterers, and although there are many ways to be relieved of sexual desire without risk, nevertheless they rush into danger! Now, isn't this sheer madness?"

"I think so," said Aristippus.

"In view of the fact that most actions essential to man are carried on in the open air, of which war and farming are not the least examples among many others, don't you think that it is a sign of great carelessness that most people are not trained to endure cold and heat?"

Aristippus agreed to this also.

"Don't you think that the man who intends to rule should train himself to endure heat and cold easily?"

"Certainly."

"If," said Socrates, "we classify the men who are self-con- *7* trolled in all these matters as fit to rule, then shall we classify the men who cannot maintain self-control as not even fit to seek for power?"

Aristippus agreed also to this.

"But now what? Since you know how to classify each of these types, have you ever considered into which category you, in all fairness, would place yourself?"

Aristippus replied, "For my part, I would never classify my- *8* self in the category of those who wish to rule. I think that I would be senseless if I added the problem of supplying the rest of the citizens with their needs! As though taking care of myself were not enough to do! It is the utmost senselessness for a man to forego many of his own wants because he is at the head of the state, and to be accountable for everything that he does not carry through when the state wishes it! States *9* think it their right to use their leaders as I use my slaves. I demand that my servants supply my needs abundantly without touching anything, and states think that their leaders ought to provide them with every good thing they can without taking anything for themselves. Anyone who wants to have a lot of trouble, and to cause others a lot of trouble, I would make fit to rule by the education you describe. As for me, I classify myself among the men who want to live as easily and pleasantly as possible!"

Socrates continued, "Would you like to consider the ques- *10* tion as to whether rulers or subjects live more pleasantly?"

"By all means!" replied Aristippus.

"First then, in Asia the Persians rule, we know; Syrians, Phrygians, and Lydians are their subjects. In Europe, the Scythians rule, while the Maeotians are their subjects. In Libya, the Carthaginians rule; the Libyans are their subjects. Which of these do you think live more pleasantly? What about the Greeks, of which you are one? Who do you think lead a pleasanter life, the ruling or the subject Greeks?"

11   "But," said Aristippus, "I do not classify myself as a slave. I think there is a middle road which I try to walk—neither the road of rulers nor that of slaves. It is the road of freedom, which leads to happiness."

12   Socrates replied, "Perhaps your statement would mean something if you added that besides not being a road of power or of slavery, it is also not a road of men! Suppose you are a human being who demands it as your right neither to rule nor be ruled, and suppose you are not willing to serve your rulers. You can, I think, see how the mighty know how to treat the weak as slaves by causing them sorrow in both their pri-
13 vate and their public affairs. Have you forgotten that men cut down grain and chop down trees which other men have sown and planted? In every way they besiege the weaker who refuse to serve them and ultimately persuade them to choose to be slaves rather than make war with stronger men. Moreover, in private life, don't you realize that the brave and powerful enslave and plunder the cowardly and weak?"

"But," said Aristippus, "to avoid suffering this, I do not confine myself to any single state; I am a foreigner everywhere."

14   Socrates exclaimed, "A very clever trick!" Not since the death of Sinis, Sciron, and Procrustes has anyone harmed a foreigner.[1] Now, however, citizens of a state pass laws in their own countries to protect themselves from injury. In addition to those they call "relations," they procure friends to aid them and they build walls for their cities. They get arms to ward off evildoers. Besides this, they arrange for allies outside of the state. Yet even those who possess all of these defenses still are

---

[1] Each of these mythological models of hospitality had his own method of murdering travelers: Sinis sought aid from passers-by in bending down trees to the earth and then released his hold so that the tree snapped back and hurled the victim to his death. Sciron kicked passers-by over a cliff when they, at his insistence, stooped over to wash his feet. Procrustes, by trimming or stretching, fitted his guests to the bed he offered them. All three were overcome by the famous Athenian hero, Theseus.

wronged. Yet you, without any defense whatsoever, spend much
time on the very roads where most people come to harm. Into
whatever state you may come, you are less than all the citizens,
and moreover you are just the sort of person to be attacked by
men bent upon evil. Do you think that because you are a foreigner, you will not suffer injury? Do you feel this confidence because the cities make proclamations of safe-conduct for you as
you come and go? Or is it that you think you would be the type
of slave which would be of no advantage to any slaveowner—
for who would want to have a man in his household who not
only enjoyed a life of luxury, but also was unwilling to work?

"Let us look, too, at the question of how masters make use
of such slaves. Don't they temper their lust by starvation, and
prevent theft by locking up the place where they can find
something to take? Don't they use chains to prevent them from
escaping, and force them out of their laziness with whips?
What do you do when you learn that one of your slaves is like
this?"

"I punish him," said Aristippus, "with every kind of evil
until I force him to submission. However, Socrates, what about
the men educated in the art of kingship—which you seem to
think is happiness? How do they differ from those who suffer
hardship from necessity if they go hungry, thirsty, cold, and
sleepless, and endure all sorts of other burdens of their own
choosing? I just don't see the difference between one and the
same back enduring the whip willingly or unwillingly; or one
and the same body besieged by all sorts of torments willingly
or unwillingly. The only difference is the senselessness of the
man who willingly endures pain."

"What, Aristippus!" exclaimed Socrates. "Don't you realize
the difference between voluntary acts of this sort and invol-
untary acts lies in the fact that the man who willingly goes
hungry, thirsty, and all the other things, may eat, drink, and so
forth whenever he wants, but the man who suffers these ills of
necessity is unable to stop them even when he wants to? Besides, the man who willingly endures discomfort is cheered by
good hope, like hunters, for instance, who toil in their hunt

19 for animals in the hope of a good catch. Such rewards for toil are really worth very little. But when it comes to those who toil to win good friends, to overcome enemies, to be strong in body and soul, to manage their homes well, to treat friends well and do good for their fatherland, how can you not help thinking that these men toil gladly for such prizes and live cheerful lives, have self-esteem and are praised and envied by 20 all others? Furthermore, laziness and pleasures of the moment never put the body into good condition, so the trainers say; they do not bring any worthwhile knowledge to the soul. Strenuous training, on the other hand, causes men to accomplish truly noble deeds, as noble men say. Somewhere [2] Hesiod says:

> It is easy to choose wickedness in abundance. The road is smooth and wickedness dwells very near. The gods have put toil and sweat in front of virtue. The path to virtue is long, steep, and rough at first. As you approach the top, the way becomes easy, although it is really difficult.

Epicharmus testifies to this in the following: 'The gods sell all goods at the price of toil.' Elsewhere he says, "Wretched man, don't seek after easy things, lest you obtain only the hard.'

21 "Prodicus the Wise, too, in his work on Heracles, which he recited to many, speaks in the same way about virtue; he says (as best as I can remember),[3] 'When Heracles was passing from boyhood to adolescence, when young men become their own masters and make clear whether they will turn in life onto the road of virtue or onto the road of evil, he went off and sat by himself in peace. He was at a loss as to which road 22 to take. He saw two tall women approaching. One was lovely to see and by nature lively and forthright. Her body was adorned with purity, her eyes with modesty, and her bearing with temperance. She wore white. The other was plump and fleshy. She had painted her face to make her complexion

---

[2] *Works and Days* 287 ff.

[3] Plato represents Socrates as referring to Prodicus of Ceus as his teacher (*Meno* 96d). Prodicus was in Athens in the last third of the fifth century. Of his most famous work entitled *The Praise of Heracles*, this quotation by Xenophon called *Heracles at the Crossroads* is all that is preserved.

whiter and redder than it really was. Her figure was gotten
up to be taller than nature had made it. Her eyes were made
up to give her a bold stare. She desired to display her beauty.
She kept looking about her to see who was looking at her, and
she often gazed at her own reflection. When they came closer   23
to Heracles, the first woman went on unchanged. The other,
eager to outdo her companion, rushed up to Heracles and
said, "I see, Heracles, that you are in doubt as to which road
to take in life. Make me your friend and I shall lead you along
the easiest and most pleasant road. No delight will go un-
tasted. You will live a life without hardship. First of all, you   24
will take no thought for wars or troubles. Instead, your concern will be what choice food or drink you should find; what
you should see or hear or touch or smell to delight you; what
youths you would most enjoy associating with; how you may
have the sweetest sleep; and how to get all this with the least
labor. Should the suspicion ever arise that you lack the power   25
to get this, don't be afraid that I will lead you through miserable discomforts of soul and body to win them! No! You will
reap the fruits of other men's work. You will keep from nothing from which you could have gain. To my associates I give
the power to profit any way and every way." When Heracles   26
heard this, he asked, "Woman, what is your name?" She said,
"My friends call me Happiness, but those who hate me dis-
parage me with the name Evil."

"'Meanwhile the other woman approached him and said,   27
"I come to you, Heracles, because I know your parents, and
because I carefully observed your character during your childhood. As a result of this, I hope that, if you take the road that
leads to me, you will become the noble doer of fine and holy
deeds and that I shall appear even more honored and more
famed for good. I shall not, however, deceive you by an introduction about pleasure. Instead I shall explain things truthfully, as the gods ordained them. The gods give men nothing   28
noble and good unless men work and toil. If you want the gods
to be propitious, you must serve the gods. If you want to be
loved by friends, you must do good to your friends. If you desire to be honored by a state, you must help the state. If you

ask to be admired by all of Greece for your virtue, you must try to aid Greece. If you wish the earth to bear fruit in abundance, you must cultivate the land. If you think that you should be enriched by cattle, you must care for the cattle. If you are eager to grow great through war and wish to be able to liberate your friends and overcome your enemies, you must learn the art of war from experienced men, and you must practice how to use it. If you want to have a strong body, you must train your body to serve your mind and exercise it with toil and sweat."

29   "Prodicus continues, 'Evil interrupted and said, "Do you realize, Heracles, how hard and long is the road to joy which this woman describes? I shall lead you along an easy and short road to happiness."

30   "'Virtue replied, "Wretched woman, what good thing do you possess? What pleasure do you know about? You are not willing to do anything to gain goodness or pleasure. You don't even wait to want pleasures, but before you feel any desire, you fill yourself full. You eat before you are hungry. You drink before you are thirsty. So as to eat pleasantly, you contrive to obtain cooks. To drink well, you prepare expensive wines and run around looking for snow in the summer. To sleep well, you not only get soft covers, but even footstools for your beds. You desire sleep not because you have worked hard, but because you have nothing to do. Before you need to, you arouse lust by every sort of means, and you use men like women. This is the way you educate your friends: by night you assault

31 them and by day you sleep away the best hours. Though you are immortal, you were cast out from the gods; you are not honored among good men. You never hear the sweetest of all sounds: praise of yourself. You never see the sweetest of all sights: your own good work. Who would believe anything you said? Who would give you anything when you need it? What sensible man would dare to be one of your band of worshipers? For when your followers are young, their bodies are weak; and when they grow older, their souls are without sense. In their youth they are sleek and brought up without work. In their old age, they are dried up and go about with great effort;

they are ashamed of what they did and are burdened with what they are doing. In their youth, they ran riot among pleasures and stored up bitter hardships for their old age.

" ' "I am a companion of the gods. I associate with good men. There is no good deed, either divine or human, without me. I am honored most of all by the gods and men to whom I am related; I am a beloved fellow worker among craftsmen, a faithful guardian of householders, a blessed protector of slaves, a good assistant in peacetime labors, a sure ally in wartime deeds, and the best partner in friendship. For my friends, the enjoyment of food and drink is pleasant and painless, because they abstain until they desire them. Their sleep is sweeter than the sleep of the idle; they are not annoyed when they wake and they do not neglect their duties because of sleep. The young rejoice in praise from their elders; the older men delight in the respect of the young. They remember with pleasure the deeds of their youth and they enjoy their present activities. Through me, they are friends of the gods; beloved by friends, honored by their native land. When their allotted end comes, they do not lie unhonored and forgotten, but they are remembered and praised forever. O Heracles, child of good parents, by such labors you can achieve the most blessed happiness." '

"This is roughly the way Prodicus pursues the theme of "The Education of Heracles by Virtue." Prodicus, however, adorned the ideas with even finer words than I have used just now. Aristippus, you ought to take this to heart and think about it. You should take thought for the life you are to lead."

Chapter 2: With Lamprocles on Filial Duty

Once, when Socrates saw his eldest son, Lamprocles, angry at his mother,[1] he said, "Tell me, son, have you ever heard certain people called ungrateful?"

[1] Xanthippe, wife of Socrates, became proverbial as a shrew in later tradition. Socrates' three sons are Lamprocles, Sophroniscus, and Menexenus.

"Of course," replied the young man.

"Do you understand what they have done to be given this bad name?"

"Yes, I do," replied Lamprocles, "They are called ungrateful because they do not repay favors when they have been well treated, although they could do so."

"Do you think that ungrateful men are considered evil-doers?" asked Socrates.

"I think so."

2   "Have you ever before examined the question as to whether it is unjust to be ungrateful to our friends and just to be ungrateful to our enemies—as in the analogous case of enslaving people, where we think it unjust to enslave our friends and just to enslave our enemies?"

"Yes, I have," replied Lamprocles. "And I think that anyone who does not try to return a favor, whether from a friend or an enemy, is unjust."

3   "If this is true, would ingratitude be simply injustice?"
His son agreed.

"Do you agree also that the greater the favor a man receives, the more unjust he is if he does not repay the favor?"
Lamprocles assented to this also.

"Could we find anyone who does more good for anyone than parents do for children? Parents bring children from nothingness into existence, to see and to share all the beauty and good which the gods offer mankind. We think that these gifts are worth everything; thus we avoid losing them at all costs. States even impose the death penalty for the most serious crimes, since they think that there is no fear of evil more effec-

4   tive in preventing injustice. Certainly you do not assume that men have children simply to gratify their lust, when the streets and dwellings are full of people who can serve that purpose? Obviously we seek the type of woman by whom we may have the best possible children, and we marry and beget children.

5   The husband, for his part, supports his wife who will bear his children, and he prepares for his future children all the benefits he thinks will be of use to them in their life. The

woman, for her part, conceives the child, carries her burden; while she is pregnant, at the risk of her life, she shares with the child the very food with which she too is nourished. She bears the child with great pain, feeds it, and takes care of it, though she has not received any good. The infant does not know who is taking such good care of it, and cannot even indicate what it wants. She, however, guesses what is good for the baby and tries to supply what it likes. She spends long hours feeding it, and patiently toils day and night without even knowing if she will receive any benefits in return. Yet it is not enough to feed children: when they seem to be capable of learning something, the parents teach them all the good they can to help them in life. If they think that someone else is more capable of teaching their children, they send them to him at great expense and take care to do everything to make their children as fine as possible."

To this the young man replied, "But even if she has done all this and much more than this, no one could stand her bad temper."

Socrates replied, "Which is harder to bear, the savage temper of a wild beast or of a mother?"

"I should say a mother's, when she is like mine!"

"Has she ever done any harm to you by biting or kicking like a wild beast?" asked Socrates.

"But, by Zeus," the young man said, "she says things that no one would ever want to hear in his whole life!"

"What about yourself? How much trouble and bother do you think you have caused her with your actions and your voice, day and night, ever since you were a small boy? How much sorrow have you brought on her by illness?"

"But I have never said or done anything to make her ashamed!" replied Lamprocles.

"What! Do you suppose it is harder for you to listen to what she says than for actors, when they say the most extreme things to each other in tragedies?"

"But they endure their threats and accusations easily, I

think, because when they speak they realize that they are not going to punish and hurt each other."

Socrates said, "You know well, not only that your mother says what she does without evil intent, but that she even wants more good things for you than for anyone else! And yet you are angry! Do you think that your mother feels malice toward you?"

"Of course not! I don't think she is malicious."

10 Socrates said, "Do you claim that she is ill-tempered, even when she has the best intentions toward you and takes care as best she can to nurse you back to health if you are sick and to see that you lack nothing; when she prays to the gods for good things for you, and pays vows to them for you? I believe that if you cannot endure such a mother, you cannot endure good things!

11 "Tell me," continued Socrates, "is there anyone else to whom you think you owe respect? Or are you ready to try to please no man and obey no general or any other leader?"

"By Zeus, I do owe respect to others, " replied Lamprocles.

12 Socrates said, "Do you want to please your neighbor, so that he will kindle a fire for you when you ask and share something with you and, if there is an accident, be willing and ready to help you?"

"Yes," said Lamprocles.

"What about this: Do you care whether or not a fellow voyager, on land or sea, or anyone else you may meet traveling, is a friend or an enemy? Do you think that you should cultivate their good will?"

"I do," he said.

13 "Then you are ready to cultivate these, but you do not think you should pay respect to your mother, who loves you most of all? Aren't you aware that the only form of ingratitude the state takes cognizance of and punishes is ingratitude toward parents? It overlooks men who fail to pay back a favor, but if a child does not pay respect to his parents, the state punishes him, rejects him, and does not permit him to hold office on the grounds that, if he sacrificed on behalf of the

state, the sacrifice would not be made out of proper respect, and that if he did something for the state, it would not be done well or justly. By Zeus, if anyone does not honor his parent's grave, the state takes cognizance of the matter in the examination of candidates for office. So, my child, if you are **14** wise, you will ask the gods for pardon if you have somehow been disrespectful of your mother. Be careful not to fall into disgrace with everyone and then be left without friends because men see you neglecting your parents. If men see that you are ungrateful toward your parents, not one of them will believe that you would ever be grateful for any favor he might do for you."

Chapter 3: With Chaerecrates on Brotherly Love

Once Socrates noticed that the two brothers, Chaerephon **1** and Chaerecrates, with whom he was acquainted, were quarreling. When he saw Chaerecrates, he said, "Tell me, Chaerecrates, you surely aren't one of those men who think that wealth is more useful than brothers? And this too, although wealth is senseless and needs assistance, while a brother has sense and can give assistance! What is more, there is a lot of wealth, but you have only one brother. This too is most amaz- **2** ing: men consider their brothers a liability because they do not possess their brothers' property, and yet do not consider their fellow citizens a loss because they do not have their fellow citizens' wealth. In the one case, men take account of the fact that living in security in a community with enough wealth is better than living alone in danger while controlling the entire wealth of the citizens. Yet in the case of brothers, they are unaware of this fact. The powerful buy slaves so as **3** to have workers and they get friends as they need help. Yet they neglect their brothers, as though friendship could arise between fellow citizens, but not between brothers. Yet the fact **4** that brothers are born of the same parents is important in friendship, and it is important as well that they are raised together—to judge from the longing that occurs even in wild beasts for the animals reared with them. Besides, other men respect those who have brothers more than those who do not, and they impose on them less."

5 Chaerecrates answered, "Socrates, if the difference were not so great, I ought perhaps to endure my brother, and not avoid him because of trifles. For even as you say, a brother who is as he should be is a good thing. But when he lacks everything and is completely the opposite of what he ought to be, why would anyone attempt the impossible?"

6 Socrates said, "Chaerecrates, can Chaerephon be as displeasing to everyone as he is to you? Or are there some who find him quite pleasant?"

"Socrates, it is just because of this that I have a right to hate him. He is pleasant to others, but whenever he is near me, everything he says and does hurts me instead of helping me."

7 "Isn't a horse the same way?" asked Socrates. "It hurts the man who tries to handle it without knowing how. So with a brother: he hurts anyone who, without knowing how, tries to deal with him."

8 "How would I not know how to deal with my brother?" replied Chaerecrates. "I know how to speak well when he speaks well and how to treat him well when he treats me well! But when he tries to annoy me in everything he says and does, I cannot speak well to him or treat him kindly, and furthermore, I won't even try to!"

9 "Your words amaze me! Chaerecrates, if you had a sheep dog that was useful with the flocks and welcomed shepherds, you would not bother to be angry even though it growled at you; rather, you would try to tame it by treating it well. Yet you say that a brother is a great good if he behaves toward you as he should. You admit, as well, that you know how to act and speak gently. You do not, however, attempt to make him be the best possible brother for you."

10 Chaerecrates said, "I fear, Socrates, that I do not have

enough wisdom to make Chaerephon behave toward me as he should."

"You don't, I think, have to devise any subtle or strange plot against him. You know, I am sure, how to win him over and bring him to esteem you."

Chaerecrates replied, "You couldn't tell me fast enough if you have observed that I know of some kind of spell which I don't realize I know!" 11

"Tell me, then," said Socrates, "if you want to get an invitation from one of your acquaintances to dine when he sacrifices, what would you do?"

"Obviously, I would first invite him to dinner when I make a sacrifice."

"If you want to persuade one of your friends to look out for your affairs while you are away, what would you do?" 12

"Obviously, I would try to do the same for him first when he is away."

"If you want to have a foreigner offer you hospitality when you come to his city, what would you do?" 13

"Obviously, I would offer him hospitality whenever he comes to Athens, and if I also wish to enlist his zeal in accomplishing the business for which I travel, obviously, I would first have to do even this for him."

"You have been concealing a knowledge of all the spells among men for a long time! Or is it," asked Socrates, "that you hesitate to take the initiative for fear that you will appear to be a coward if you are first to treat your brother well? Yet a man seems worthy of the highest praise who anticipates his enemies' evildoing and his friends' benefactions. If I thought that Chaerephon would be better able than you to take the lead in this reconciliation, I would be trying to persuade him to make you a friend. Now, however, you seem more likely to accomplish this, if you take the lead." 14

Chaerecrates replied, "Socrates, what you say astonishes me. It is not like you to tell me, the younger of the two brothers, to take the lead! Everyone believes just the opposite of this! The elder brother should be first to speak and act." 15

16 "How is that?" said Socrates. "Isn't it always the custom for the younger to give way to his elder when they meet, to offer his seat, to honor him with the soft place, and to yield in conversation? Don't hesitate, sir, but try to pacify the man and very quickly he will listen to you. Don't you see how ambitious and sincere he is? You may catch wicked men with bribes—there is no better way!—but you prevail over truly noble men by being friendly."

17 "But what if he doesn't change for the better when I do this?" asked Chaerecrates.

"What risk do you run," replied Socrates, "except that of proving that you are good and you love your brother, while he is base and not worth helping? Yet this, I think, won't happen. I believe that he will vie to outdo you in kindness in all he says and does when he sees that you invite him to the

18 contest. As it is now, you two are like the two hands which the god made to help one another, but which neglect their function and are diverted to thwarting one another, or like the two feet which are created by divine fate to work together

19 but which disregard this and get in each other's way. Would it not be great ignorance and misfortune to use for a harmful purpose something that was created for a good purpose? As I understand it, god made two brothers to be of much greater use to one another than two hands, two feet, two eyes, or the other pairs of things he created for mankind. Hands, if they had to do anything together more than an arm's length away, could not do so; feet could do nothing more than a stride apart. Though eyes seem to have the longest range, they could not at the same time look both in front and behind at objects that are quite near to one another. Two brothers who are friends, even though they are very far apart, can still be of great help to one another."

Chapter 4: A Discourse on Friendship

1 Once I heard Socrates speaking on friendship in a way that would be most beneficial to anyone in winning and in

dealing with friends. He said that he had heard many men say that the greatest of all possessions was a sincere and good friend. "Yet," he said, "the masses are careful in everything except acquiring a friend. I see them taking great care in acquiring houses, fields, slaves, cattle, and furniture, and in trying to keep what they have. As for a friend, which they say is the greatest good, I see the masses paying no attention to how to acquire a friend or how to keep the friends they have. When their friends and their slaves are sick, I see them calling the doctor for their slaves and carefully doing everything else for their slaves' health, all the while ignoring their friends. If both friends and slave die, they are grieved at the death of the slave and feel the loss. At their friend's death, however, they don't feel that they have lost anything. They never allow any of their other possessions to go uncared for or unattended. Only their friends lack the necessary care! I have found, besides, that the masses know just how much they possess, even when they have a great deal. Yet these same men are not only unaware of the number of their friends, though they are few, but even when they try to list their friends for someone who asks, they add names of friends, then remove them again. This is how much they care about friends!

"Yet, when compared to anything else, wouldn't a good friend appear to be a greater possession? What horse, what yoke of oxen, is as useful as a useful friend? What slave is as kind or steadfast? What other possession is so versatile? For a good friend puts himself at his friend's disposal against loss of every kind, whether in private business or in public affairs. When the need arises, a good friend gives support, and when fear troubles, he gives aid. Sometimes he shares expenses, sometimes work; at times he uses persuasion; at times, force. A good friend is often cheered to see his friends prosperous; often he helps them up again when they stumble. If his hands may serve, or his eyes foresee or his ears anticipate something or his feet run anywhere, a friend lags behind none in his generosity. A friend often does for a friend what the friend did not complete, see, hear, or finish for himself. Although some men try to cultivate trees for the fruit they bear, yet when it comes to man's most fruitful possession, which is called 'a good friend,' most men are slow and neglectful in their care."

Chapter 5: With Antisthenes on the Value of Friends

1   I once heard still another discussion by Socrates which, I thought, persuaded the hearer to ask himself how much he was worth to his friends. For Socrates had noticed one of his companions neglecting a friend who was hard pressed by poverty, and he asked Antisthenes in the presence of many other

2   listeners including the neglectful man, "Antisthenes, do friends, like slaves, have a value? For example, one slave is worth two minas, another not even half a mina. This slave may be worth five minas, and this one ten. Nicias, son of Nicerates, is said to have purchased an overseer for his silver mine for a talent. So I am examining the question, do friends have values as slaves do?"

3   "By Zeus," said Antisthenes, "I would rather have this man as a friend than have two minas; while I would not take half a mina for that man. I might prefer someone to ten minas and for another I would pay any price in money or trouble to have him as my friend!"

4   "Then," said Socrates, "if this is so, a man would do well to ask himself how much he happens to be worth to his friends and to try to be worth as much as possible so that his friends will not betray him. I often hear complaints like this: 'A friend has betrayed me,' or 'A man I thought was my friend

5   preferred a mina to me.' When I investigate all such complaints, I discover that perhaps he was tempted to sell a wicked friend when it was possible to get more than he was worth, like the slave owner who sells a wicked slave and takes anything he can get. I observe that good slaves are not put up for sale at all, and that good friends are not betrayed."

Chapter 6: With Critobulus on How to Win Friends

In the following discussion, Socrates taught us, I think, how *1* to test which friends are worth winning. He said, "Critobulus, tell me this: if we should need a good friend, how would we try to find one? Should we first see who controls his appetite, thirst, lust, and his inclination to sleep and to do nothing? For a man enslaved by these could not do what must be done for himself or his friends!"

"By Zeus, surely not!" replied Critobulus.

"Do you think that we should avoid a man dominated by these?"

"Certainly."

"What about the spendthrift? He never has enough, but *2* always needs his neighbors' goods; once he gets them, he can never pay them back, yet when he fails to get them, he hates the man who refused him. Don't you think that this type makes a difficult friend?"

"Absolutely!"

"Should he also be avoided?"

"He must be," said Critobulus.

"What about the man who is skilled in business dealings, *3* who wants a lot of money and is therefore difficult to bargain with; who takes pleasure in getting and is unwilling to pay back?"

"He seems to be more wicked than the other!" replied Critobulus.

"What about the man who loves business so much that he *4* has leisure for nothing except what gives him some profit?"

"He too must be avoided, I think. He would be useless to a friend."

"What, then, of the troublemaker who wishes to provide his friends with many enemies?" asked Socrates.

"We must, by Zeus, avoid him." replied Critobulus.

"What if a man has none of these faults, but allows himself

to accept kindness without thinking at all of returning the good deed?"

"He too would be useless. But Socrates, what sort of man should we try to make friends with?"

5   "The man who is the opposite of these, I think: who has self-control over the pleasures of the body, who happens to be benevolent, honest in business, and eager to compete in a contest of good deeds so as to be of use to his friends!"

6   "How should we test these qualities, Socrates, before we become intimate?"

"The same way we test sculptors. We don't judge them by their words, but when we see that a sculptor has made fine statues in the past, we trust that he will make good statues in the future."

7   "Do you mean that a man who, it appears, has treated his friends well, will obviously help his new friends also?"

Socrates replied, "Yes, it is the same with horses. I see that a man who has always treated his horses well will treat the others well also."

8   "May it be so! Suppose we think that a man is worth having as a friend. How should we make friends with him?"

"First you should ask the advice of the gods as to whether they advise making friends with him."

"Then what do we do if we think that the gods do not oppose it? Can you say how he should be hunted?"

9   "By Zeus," replied Socrates, "not by pursuit, like a rabbit, or by cunning, like birds, or by force, like enemies! It is a difficult task to capture an unwilling friend, and very hard also to keep him a prisoner like a slave. For those experiencing this become enemies, not friends."

"How, then, do we make friends?"

10   "They say there are spells that those who know can chant so as to make friends of whomever they want. There are love charms too, which experts use to make people want them as friends."

11   "Where could we learn these?"

"You have heard from Homer the spell the Sirens sang to

Odysseus. This is its beginning: 'Come here, famed Odysseus, great glory of the Achaeans.' " [1]

"Is this the spell, Socrates, that the Sirens sang to catch other men so that they were spellbound and could not leave?"

"No. They sang this only to those who were ambitious for virtue." 12

"Do you mean," asked Critobulus, "that they must sing to each man a spell which he will believe to be praise, not mockery, when he hears it?"

"Yes; for a man would only be more hated and would drive men off if he told a person who knew he was short, ugly, and weak that he was tall, handsome, and strong."

"Do you know any other spells?"

"No, but I have heard that Pericles knew many which he sang to the state to win its friendship." [2] 13

"How did Themistocles make the state love him?"

"By Zeus, not by spells; by encircling it with good defenses." [3]

"Do you mean, Socrates, that if we intend to make a good friend, we must be good in all we say and do?" asked Critobulus. 14

"Do you think that you can be evil and still have good friends?"

"I have seen," replied Critobulus, "poor rhetoricians who are friends of good public speakers and generals whose companions are incapable of being generals." 15

"But to stay on the subject of our discussion: do you believe that useless people can become useful friends?" 16

"No, of course not! But if an evil man cannot have truly noble friends, then I want to know this also: can a man who has become truly noble easily be a friend of truly noble people?"

"What bothers you, Critobulus, is that you have often seen 17

---

1 *Odyssey* 12. 184.
2 Pericles was considered the most eloquent orator of his time.
3 I.e., with ships and fortifications.

men who do good and avoid evil keep one another at a distance instead of being friends, and treat each other worse than worthless men."

18   "Not only private citizens do this," replied Critobulus, "but states as well. States can seek to do right and have no liking
19   for evil, yet often they are hostile to one another. When I realize this, I am quite discouraged about ever having friends. I know that evil men cannot be friends to one another. How could ungrateful, careless, greedy, faithless, intemperate men become friends? It seems to me that evil men are by nature
20   utter enemies of one another, rather than friends! But as you say, evil men could not ever make friends with good men. How could evildoers become friends of men who hate evil? If men who seek virtue fight over the leadership of the state and through envy despise each other, who will be left to be friends and where will we find kindness and loyalty among men?"

21   "But, Critobulus," said Socrates, "this is somewhat complicated. Men have by nature some friendly elements. For instance, they need one another and they sympathize with each other and, by working together, aid each other; and, since they are conscious of this, they are grateful to one another. They have, on the other hand, some hostile elements. For instance, when they consider the same things fine and pleasant, they fight for them. They hold varying opinions and oppose one another. Strife and anger are hostile, covetousness is ma-
22   levolent, and envy is hateful. Nevertheless, friendship slips past all these pitfalls and unites truly noble men. Because of their virtue, men choose to have moderate means without trouble rather than to be master of everything through war. Though they are hungry and thirsty, they can share without a pang their food and drink; and although they enjoy sexual delights, they can forego them so as not to bother someone
23   whom they should not bother. They are able not only to share their wealth lawfully without covetousness, but also to lend one another money. They can settle a dispute without ill will— indeed, even to each other's advantage—and they can prevent anger from growing into something they will regret. They are

completely above envy; they give their own goods to their friends
and treat the goods of their friends as they would their own.
Isn't it reasonable that truly noble men share political honors   *24*
not only without injury to each other but even with advantage
to one another? When men want to be honored in states and
to be leaders so as to have the power to steal money, coerce
men, and live luxuriously, they will be unjust, unscrupulous,
and incapable of making friends with anyone. On the other
hand, if a man wishes to be honored in his state so that he   *25*
may avoid suffering injustices himself and can help his friends
obtain justice, if when he becomes a leader he tries to do good
for his fatherland, why could he not be a friend to another
man like himself? Will he be less capable of aiding his friends
who are among the truly noble men? Will he be less able to
help the state because he has the cooperation of truly noble
men? Even in gymnastic contests, it is obvious that, if all the   *26*
strongest came on the same side against the weaker, they
would win all the events and take all the prizes. This is not
permitted in the games. In politics, on the other hand, in
which the truly noble men are in control, no one prevents
anyone from giving aid to the state. How then is it not great
gain for a man who has the noblest friends, and who uses them
as partners in his activities rather than as rivals, to engage in
politics? Also, it is obvious that the man who wages war needs   *27*
allies; the man who fights against truly noble men will need
them even more. Men who are willing to be allies must be
well treated so that they may be willing to work hard. It is far
better to do good to a few good men than to a lot of evil men.
The unscrupulous want many more favors than the good. But
cheer up, Critobulus," continued Socrates, "try to become   *28*
good. Then try to catch truly noble friends. Perhaps I could
aid you somehow in your hunt for truly noble friends, for I
am skilled in love. When I desire them, I become completely
absorbed in making them return my friendship and longing.
I desire their company, and I want them to desire mine. You   *29*
too will feel the need of this, I see, when you want to make
friends. Don't conceal the identity of the men you want as

friends; for I am quite skilled in hunting men, since I take great care to please those who please me."

30 Critobulus replied, "Socrates, these are lessons I have long wished for, especially if the same skill is useful to me for winning souls among good men and winning bodies among beautiful men!"

31 "Critobulus," retorted Socrates, "it is impossible, with my skill, to force beautiful men to submit to me. I am sure that the reason men avoided Scylla is that she laid her hands on them. The Sirens touched no one, but sang for all from afar. Thus it is, they say, that all submit to them and when they hear them they are bewitched."

32 Critobulus replied, "I don't intend to lay hands on anyone. If you have a good method of winning friends, teach it to me."

"You don't intend to bring mouth to mouth either?"

"Don't worry," said Critobulus, "I won't put my mouth on anyone's mouth unless he is beautiful."

"Right away," said Socrates, "you have spoken completely to your disadvantage! The beautiful will not submit to such things. The ugly, however, like it because they believe that they are called beautiful because of their souls."

33 Critobulus said, "I shall give one kiss to the beautiful and a thousand kisses to the good; cheer up, then, and teach me the art of hunting friends!"

"Then, Critobulus, when you want to win a friend, will you let me give him warning that you admire him and desire to be his friend?"

"Warn him then," said Critobulus, "for I know that no one hates a man who praises him."

34 "If I warn him also," said Socrates, "that you admire him and feel kindly toward him, you won't think I am slandering you, will you?"

"Of course not: I myself feel kindly toward those whom I suppose to feel kindly toward me."

35 Socrates said, "I may then say this about you to those whom you want to be your friends. Furthermore, give me permission to say also that you take care of your friends and delight in

no one more than in good friends; that you are as overjoyed at your friends' good works as you are at your own; that you delight in the prosperity of friends no less than in your own, and you never tire of working on your friends' behalf; that you know that human virtue consists of surpassing friends in doing good and enemies in doing harm. This way I think you will find me a useful companion in your hunt for good friends."

"Why," said Critobulus, "do you speak as if you were not   36
free to say about me whatever you want to say?"

"But I am not, to judge by what I have heard Aspasia [4] say. She said that good matchmakers were shrewd in arranging marriages for men if they reported good qualities truthfully and refused to praise men falsely; for the deceived parties hate each other and the matchmaker as well. I am convinced that this is correct and I believe I cannot say anything in praise of you without verifying it first."

"Socrates, you are the kind of friend who will help me find   37
friends if I am at all fit to have them. If I should not be fit, then you would not be willing to make up something to say so as to help me."

"How do you think I can help you most, Critobulus? By praising you falsely or by persuading you to try to become a good man? If you are not sure of the answer, examine the   38
following examples. Suppose I wanted to make a shipowner your friend, and to do so I falsely praised you by alleging that you were a good navigator. Suppose he believed me and put you in charge of his ship, when you know nothing about navigating. Would you have any hope of not destroying both yourself and the ship? Or, suppose that by lying publicly I persuaded the state to entrust itself to you by making you a general or a judge or a statesman? What do you think would be your fate, or the fate of the state because of you? If I lie about your being a businessman and in this way privately persuade some citizens to put their business in your hands,

[4] Aspasia of Miletus came to Athens to study rhetoric. There she became the mistress of the statesman Pericles.

39 wouldn't you, when put to the test, only ruin them and appear ridiculous? The quickest, surest, and best road to being considered good in something is to try to be good in something. If you only look, you will find that all the things called virtues in man increase with study and practice. Therefore, Critobulus, I think that we must try to follow [5] this, but if you don't agree, tell me."

"I would be ashamed, Socrates, to disagree with this. If I did, I would be not speaking either the truth, or any good at all."

Chapter 7: Socrates Solves Aristarchus' Problems

1 In regard to our next subject, the troubles that bothered his friends: when they arose from ignorance, he tried to cure them by advice; when they arose from need, he taught his friends to help one another according to their resources. I shall relate what I know about Socrates on this subject.

One day he saw Aristarchus looking very gloomy. "Aristarchus," he said, "you are obviously troubled by something. You must share your troubles with your friends. We might be able to lighten your load."

2 "Socrates," said Aristarchus, "I am in great difficulty. When the revolution [1] occurred and many fled to the Piraeus, my sisters and nieces and cousins who were left behind came to my house, so that there are fourteen living in my house, not counting the slaves. We get no income from the land because our enemies have seized it. We get nothing from the rent because no one is living in the city. No one is buying portable property and it is impossible to borrow money anywhere—I think it would be easier to find money in the streets than to borrow it! Socrates, it is hard to watch my relatives being

[5] The verb that Socrates actually used is lost from the manuscript.

[1] The popular uprising led by Thrasybulus against the Thirty Tyrants (404 B.C.).

ruined, but impossible to support so many under such difficult conditions."

When Socrates heard this, he said, "How can it be that   *3*
Ceramon, who has many to support, can supply not only his
own needs, but even those of his relatives, yet is still saving
enough to be rich? You, on the other hand, have many to support and you are afraid that you will be ruined by poverty."

"Because, by Zeus, he supports slaves. I support free men."

"Which are better: your free men or Ceramon's slaves?"   *4*
asked Socrates.

"Of course I think my free men are better!"

"Isn't it a shame that he is wealthy because of his slave
household, while you are poor though your household is much
nobler!"

"Yes, by Zeus! He supports craftsmen, but I support a
liberally educated household."

"What are craftsmen? Those who know how to produce   *5*
something useful?" asked Socrates.

"Yes."

"Are groats useful?"

"Exceedingly useful," replied Aristarchus.

"What about bread?" asked Socrates.

"Just as useful!"

"Then what about men's and women's cloaks, tunics, mantles, and vests?"

"All these are very useful."

"Then," continued Socrates, "don't your relatives know how
to make any of these products?"

"I think they can make them all."

"Don't you realize that from one of these products, groats,   *6*
Nausicydes not only supports himself, his household, and his
swine and cattle as well, but even has enough left to perform
duties for his state frequently? From baking bread, Cyrebus
feeds his whole family and lives in luxury. Demes of Collytus
lives from producing mantles; Menon from making cloaks.
Most Megarians make their living from manufacturing vests."

"Yes, by Zeus!" said Aristarchus. "For they buy foreign

slaves and force them to make good products. But I have free men and relatives in my household."

7   "Do you think, then, that because they are free men and related to you they ought not to do anything except eat and sleep? Do you find men who live an idle life any better than the other free men? Do you consider them happier than men who are engaged in crafts which they know are useful for a livelihood? Do you think that, on the one hand, idleness and carelessness aid men to learn what they should know, to remember what they have learned, to be healthy and strong in body, and to get and keep the things that are useful and beneficial in life? Do you think that industry and care, on the

8   other hand, are useless? Did the women of your household learn skills that have had no practical application and are useless? Or did they learn them for the opposite reason: to use these skills and to benefit from them? How would men be more likely to be temperate—by being idle or by using their skills? How, more just—by working or by idly discussing the necessities of life? But also I can well imagine that you don't

9   love these ladies, nor they you. You think they are a burden, and they perceive that you feel burdened. As a result, it is likely that the burden will become greater and their previous gratitude will diminish. If you keep them busy, you will love them, and when they see they are useful to you, they will love you. When they see that you are pleased with them, you will both remember the benefits of the past more pleasantly, and will feel increasing gratitude as a result. You will, therefore,

10   be kinder and more at home with each other. If, of course, they were about to do something disgraceful, they ought to prefer death. As it is now, however, they know what is the finest and most fitting work for women and they all would do easily, quickly, well, and most gladly what they know how to do. Do not hesitate to give them work which will profit both you and them. Probably they will obey willingly."

11   "By the gods!" said Aristarchus, "I am so sure you are right that while I previously would not venture to borrow, knowing I would spend what I got without being able to pay it back, now I think I'll borrow capital for work for them."

As a result, the capital was supplied and wool purchased; *12*
they ate their noonday meal as they worked, and stopped work
only at supper time. They were cheerful instead of gloomy,
and smiled at each other instead of glowering. They loved
Aristarchus as their guardian, and he loved them because
they were useful. Finally, Aristarchus came to Socrates and
joyfully told him the tale, adding that they even reproached
him for being the only one in the house who didn't work for
his food. Socrates said, "Then why don't you tell them the   *13*
tale of the dog? The story goes that when animals could talk,
a ewe said to her master, 'You do a very strange thing. You
give us nothing except what the land yields us, while we furnish you with wool, lambs, and cheese. Yet you give your dog
part of your own food, and the dog doesn't give you nearly
as much as we do.' The dog heard and replied, 'By Zeus,   *14*
I do so! I keep you sheep from being stolen by men or
snatched away by wolves. If I didn't guard you, you wouldn't
be able even to feed; instead you would live in constant fear
of perishing.' Thus the dog spoke, and the sheep agreed that
the dog should be preferred. Tell the women yourself that like
the dog, you are their guard and caretaker; because of you
they cannot be harmed by anyone, and they can work and
live safely and pleasantly."

Chapter 8: Socrates Advises Eutherus on Finding Suitable Employment

Once Socrates saw a former companion whom he had not [1]
seen for a long time and said, "Eutherus, where did you appear from?"

"After the end of the war,[1] Socrates, we returned from
abroad and are now here. Since we lost our foreign possessions
and my father left me nothing in Attica, I have returned
home and am forced now to make a living as a laborer. I

[1] That is, at the end of the Peloponnesian War (spring 404 B.C.), when
Athens lost her colonial possessions.

think this is better than asking someone for money, especially since I have nothing to borrow against."

2   "How long do you think your body will be strong enough to work like this for a living?"

"By Zeus, not very long!"

"When you get older, clearly you will need money, but no one will want to pay you for your labor."

"You are right."

3   "Then it would be better to devote yourself to the kind of work which will be fruitful even when you are old. Offer yourself to someone who has more money and who needs a partner. Oversee his business, gather his crops, and look after his property. Get a return for your services."

4   "Socrates, it would be hard to endure servitude."

"Yet the rulers of states and the guardians of public affairs are not considered slaves on account of this. They are considered to have even more freedom."

5   "In short, Socrates, I will not allow myself to be accountable to anyone."

"But Eutherus, it is not easy to find work for which you don't have to give an account. It is difficult to do anything without a mistake, and difficult to escape unfair criticism even when you have made no mistakes. I wonder if it is so easy to escape blame even for the work in which you are now em-

6   ployed. You must try to avoid faultfinders and look for fair-minded men. Undertake duties which you are strong enough to complete; beware of those you cannot do. Whatever you take on, give it your best and most wholehearted attention. This way you will find, I think, the least possible blame; you will find aid for your troubles and live most easily, comfortably, and amply even in your old age."

Chapter 9: The Case of Archedemus and Crito

1   I know that once Socrates heard Crito say how difficult life in Athens was for the man who wanted to mind his own

business. "Even now," Crito continued, "men are bringing lawsuits against me, not because they have been wronged by me, but because they think that I would rather pay them than have trouble."

Socrates said, "Tell me, Crito, do you feed dogs to keep wolves from your flocks?" 2

"Of course, since it is more profitable to feed them than not."

"Why don't you support a man who would be willing and able to ward off the men who try to hurt you?"

"I would gladly do so if I were not afraid that he, too, 3 might turn against me."

"Don't you realize that it is much more pleasant to profit by pleasing a man like you than by quarreling with him? Surely you know there are men in this city who are ambitious to have you as their friend?"

As a result of this conversation they looked up Archedemus, 4 who was a very able orator and businessman, but was poor. He was not the type of man to make profits in just any way at all. He was honest and used to say that it was the easiest thing to get money from false accusers. Whenever Crito collected grain, oil, wine, or wool or some other useful crop, he put some aside and gave it to Archedemus. Whenever he sacrificed, he invited Archedemus and took care of him at all such occasions. Archedemus came to consider Crito's home a place 5 of refuge and treated Crito with exceeding respect. Immediately he uncovered the many crimes of Crito's false accusers, and their many enemies. He summoned one to court on penalty of fine or imprisonment. The defendant, aware of his 6 numerous crimes, did everything to get free of Archedemus, but Archedemus could not be shaken loose until the defendant let Crito alone and gave him money. When Archedemus 7 had been involved in this and several similar cases, soon it was like the case of the shepherd who had the good dog: the other shepherds wanted to pasture their herds near him so as to enjoy the benefit of his dog. Thus many of his friends asked Crito to let Archedemus protect them. Archedemus 8 gladly helped Crito and not only Crito was left in peace, but his friends [1] were also. If anyone whom Archedemus had offended reproached him with flattering Crito in order to get favors, Archedemus would ask, "Which is disgraceful: to exchange favors with good men, and to make good men your friends and quarrel with evil men? Or to try to harm truly noble men, treat them as enemies, and help evil men, and to treat evil men as friends and prefer them to good ones?" From then on, Archedemus was a friend to Crito, and was honored by all Crito's other friends.

Chapter 10: The Case of Diodorus and Hermogenes

1   I know also of the following discussion between Socrates and a companion, Diodorus.

"Tell me, Diodorus, if one of your servants runs away, do you take the trouble to bring him back safely?"

2   "Of course, by Zeus! I even get others to help by offering a reward."

"What of this?" continued Socrates. "If one of your servants is ill, do you take care of him and summon a doctor to prevent his death?"

"By all means!"

"Suppose one of your friends who is much more useful than your servants is in danger of being ruined by poverty. Do you
3   think it worth your while to save him? Surely you know that Hermogenes is a sensible man and would be ashamed not to pay back any help you give him. Yet when a man is a willing servant, kind, steadfast, and able to do what he is ordered—not only that, but even able to take the initiative, to have foresight, and to give advice—he is worth many servants. Good
4   householders, indeed, do their buying at a time when they can buy valuable products for a small price. Under the circumstances, you can now get good loyal friends."

[1] Archedemus is the formidable prosecutor who brought the charges against the generals who fought at Arginusae. See note 8, page 7.

Diodorus said, "You are right, Socrates. Tell Hermogenes   5
to come to me."

"Not I, by Zeus!" replied Socrates, "for I don't think it is
any better for you to send for him than for you to go to him
yourself. Furthermore, the good accomplished by doing this is
no greater for him than it is for you." So Diodorus went to   6
Hermogenes, and by paying him a small amount acquired a
friend who watched to see what he could say or do to aid and
please Diodorus.

BOOK THREE

HOW SOCRATES WAS A GOOD INFLUENCE ON HIS FRIENDS

Chapter 1: The Qualifications and Duties of a General

1   I shall now tell how Socrates, by making men careful about what to strive for, helped them in their quest for honors. Once, when he heard that Dionysodorus [1] had come to the city and professed to teach how to be a general, he talked with one of his followers who, he realized, wished to win this honor in

2   Athens. "It is really a shame, young man, for a man who wants to be a general in Athens to neglect the study of how to be a general, when he has it in his power to learn this art. It would be more just for the state to fine him than to fine someone for contracting to make a statue when he has not learned how.

3   For amid the dangers of war, the state is entrusted to the general completely, and the good likely to result if he succeeds, or the evil if he fails, is enormous. It would be quite just to fine the man who neglects to learn this art and worries only about getting votes!"

    By speaking this way Socrates persuaded him to go and learn.

4   After the young man had studied and returned to Socrates, Socrates teased him and said, "Don't you think, gentlemen, that this young man, now that he has learned to be a general, appears more majestic? Like Homer's 'Majestic Agamemnon'? Like a man who has learned to play the cithara and hence is

[1] Dionysodorus came to Athens from Chios. He is pictured as incompetent in Plato's *Euthyphro*.

a citharist whether or not he plays, or the man who has learned to heal and is a doctor whether or not he heals, so from now on he will continue to be a general, even if no one votes for him! On the other hand, the man who does not know how, can never be a general or a doctor, even if he gets all the votes. Still," Socrates continued, "in case one of us should be a commander of a squadron or of a company under you, tell us how Dionysodorus began to teach you how to be a general, so that we may be more knowledgeable in military matters."

5

The young man replied, "He began at the same point at which he ended: He taught me tactics and nothing else."

"But," said Socrates, "that is only a small part of being a general! A general must be fully prepared to furnish the equipment necessary for war. He must be ready with supplies for the troops. He must be inventive, industrious, careful of his men, hardy, shrewd, both kind and cruel, both straightforward and devious, both a watchman and a thief. He must be lavish and rapacious, generous and grasping, cautious and yet quick to attack—to name some of the many qualities which a good general must have, either through nature or through acquired knowledge. Tactics are fine and the army drawn up in battle positions is far better than the army not posted in battle positions. Similarly, stones, mud bricks, wood, and tile scattered about in disorder are no use at all; yet when they are arranged so that the materials do not rot and decay—when the stones and tile are on the top and bottom, that is, with the mud bricks and wood in the middle—just as in building, then there results that worthwhile structure which we call a house."

6

7

"Socrates," said the young man, "you have drawn a very apt analogy, for in war the best soldiers must be placed in the front line and in the rear, with the poorest ones in between, to be led by the one or pushed by the other."

8

"That is fine," said Socrates, "if he taught you to discriminate between good and evil men. Otherwise, what is the use of what you learned? If he bade you to put the good silver

9

coins on the top and bottom and the base silver coins in between, and failed to teach you to discriminate between the good and the base silver, he would not be helping you at all."

"By Zeus, he did not teach me that! I would have to discriminate between the good and evil men myself."

10   "Why don't we consider," said Socrates, "how we might avoid mistaking them?"

"Please," replied the young man.

"Then," said Socrates, "suppose we must carry off money, would we be correct to station the men who love money most in the front?"

"I think so."

"Suppose there is danger to face. Should we place the men who love honor most in the front?"

"Yes, because they are willing to face danger for the sake of praise. These would not be hard to find, but could be selected easily, since they are completely obvious."

11   "But did he teach you only to draw up men into battle positions? Or did he also teach you where and how each formation must be used?"

"Not at all!"

"But there are many different situations; one ought not to draw up or lead troops in the same way for all of them."

"He did not, however, make this clear."

"By Zeus," said Socrates, "go back and ask him again. For if he knows this—unless he is shameless—he will be ashamed to have taken your money and to have sent you away still ignorant."

Chapter 2: Advice to a General-Elect

1   Once Socrates happened to meet a man who had been elected general and said, "Why do you think Homer called Agamemnon 'the shepherd of the people'?[1] Isn't it because a shepherd must see to it that his sheep are safe and have food,

---

[1] *Iliad* II. 243.

and that the object for which they are raised is obtained; while a general too must see to it that his soldiers are safe and have supplies, and that the goal for which they are in the army will be attained? Now, they serve in the army so as to overcome the enemy and become more prosperous. Why did he praise Agamemnon with these words, 'Both a good king and a sturdy warrior'? [2] Isn't it because he would be a 'sturdy warrior,' not because he fights well by himself against the enemy, but rather because he arouses bravery throughout all the camp? Wouldn't he be a 'good king,' not because he takes good care only of his own livelihood, but because he brings prosperity to the men over whom he is king? A king is chosen not to take good care of himself, but so that the men who chose him may prosper. All serve in the army so as to get the best possible life, and they choose generals for the purpose of leading them to this goal. Therefore, the general must accomplish this for those who have elected him general. It is not easy to find anything finer than this goal, or anything more disgraceful than its opposite." In examining what the qualities of a good leader are, Socrates reduced leadership to the ability to bring prosperity to one's followers.

Chapter 3: A Conversation with a Hipparch

Once, I know, he spoke like this to a man who had been elected hipparch: [1] "Could you tell us, young man, why ever you wanted to be a hipparch? Surely, not so as to march at the head of the cavalry. The mounted archers demand this as their right and they march ahead of even the hipparchs."

"You are right," he replied.

"But it is not really so as to become known to everyone. Even madmen are known to everyone."

2 *Iliad* III. 179.
1 In Athens, there were two cavalry leaders, hipparchs, who were subordinate to the ten generals. Xenophon wrote a treatise on this office. See Introduction, pp. xxi, xxiii.

2   "That also is true," replied the young man.

"Is it because you think that you would improve the cavalry, then hand it over to the state, and that if ever the need should arise for the cavalry, as their leader you would become the cause of good to the state?"

"Yes, indeed."

"By Zeus," said Socrates, "that's fine, if you can do it. But if I am right, the office to which you have been elected has charge of the horses as well as the horsemen."

"Yes," replied the young man.

3   "Come! Tell us just how you intend to improve the horses!"

"But that is not my job! Each man must take care of his own horse by himself."

4   "But," said Socrates, "suppose they come to you with horses that are so lame, with such bad legs, or so weak and so underfed that they cannot keep pace, or so wild that they will not stay in position as you order, or such bad kickers that they cannot be got in position? What good will the cavalry be to you? How can you, as their leader, do any good for the state?"

"You are right," replied the young man. "I shall try to take care of the horses as best as I can."

5   "Next, won't you try to improve the horsemen as well?"

"Of course I shall."

"Won't you first make them more expert in mounting their horses?"

"Yes, I must," he replied, "so that if any one of them is thrown from his horse, he may have a better chance of saving himself."

6   "Next, suppose the cavalry must face danger. Would you command them to meet the enemy on sandy ground where you are used to riding, or would you try to drill in the kind of country where wars take place?"

"The second is better," replied the young man.

7   "Next! Will you be concerned with unhorsing as many of the enemy as possible?"

"This too is a rather good course," replied the young man.

"Do you plan to arouse and enrage the horsemen against the enemy, so as to make them more brave?"

"I had not planned to. But now I shall try."

"Have you thought at all about how the horsemen will obey you? For, unless they obey, there is no use having good horses and brave horsemen."

"You are right, Socrates. How can one exhort them to obey?"

"Surely you know this. In everything, men are most willing to obey those whom they consider best. For example, in sickness, they obey the doctor they consider the most skilled; on a ship, sailors obey the best navigator, in farming, the best farmer."

"Yes, indeed," replied the young man.

"Isn't it most reasonable," continued Socrates, "that even in horsemanship, others are most willing to obey the man who appears to know the most about what must be done?"

"Socrates, if then I am obviously the best among them, will this fact suffice to make them obey me?"

"Yes," replied Socrates, "if, in addition, you teach them that it will be better and safer for them to obey you."

"How, indeed, shall I teach them this?"

"By Zeus," said Socrates, "that is much easier than having to teach them that evil is better and more profitable than good!"

"Do you mean," said the young man, "that a hipparch must, in addition to the other things, take care to be able to speak?"

"Do you think," said Socrates, "that a hipparch should be silent? Haven't you realized that all we have learned to be best as prescribed by law (and through this we indeed know how to live), we have learned through the medium of speech? Indeed, everyone learns all good lessons through speech. The best teachers use words the best, and those who best know the most important things argue the best. Don't you realize that when Athens sends a chorus to a contest, as for example in Delos, no group from anywhere else can match it? Athens' manhood is unrivaled."

13   "You are right."

"It isn't that the Athenians are superior to the others in sweetness of voice or in size and beauty of body. They excel in the love of honor, which best spurs them on toward noble and honorable deeds."

"This also is true," replied the young man.

14   "If a man takes pains even with the cavalry here, don't you think that the Athenians would far excel others in their cavalry, not only in equipment and horses, but also in discipline and readiness to face the perils of the enemy, if they thought they would receive praise and honor by doing this?"

"It is likely."

15   "Therefore don't hesitate! Try to exhort your men to do the things from which you yourself will profit, and, through you, your fellow citizens."

"By Zeus, I will try!"

Chapter 4: Consolation to an Unsuccessful Candidate in an Election

1   Once Socrates saw Nichomachides leaving the polls. He asked, "Who were elected generals, Nichomachides?"

Nichomachides replied, "Socrates, isn't it like the Athenians that they did not elect me? I have been on the lists and worn myself out in military service as a company and squadron commander. I have been wounded so many times by the enemy." He uncovered the scars of his wounds. "Yet they elected Antisthenes, who has never been on a campaign even as a hoplite, and has done nothing very special in the cavalry. He doesn't know how to do anything except make money!"

2   "Isn't that a good recommendation, especially if he is able to get supplies for the soldiers?" replied Socrates.

"Businessmen can make money," said Nichomachides, but that is not enough to make them good generals!"

Socrates continued, "Antisthenes, however, likes to win, and this is a must for a general. Don't you see how often he has been choregus and has always produced winning choruses?" *3*

"By Zeus!" said Nichomachides, "There is no similarity at all between paying the expenses of a chorus and leading an army."

"Antisthenes was not experienced in teaching singing or training choruses, yet he was able to find experts who could," Socrates replied. *4*

"And," said Nichomachides, "as general, then, he will find some to give orders and others to fight for him."

Socrates replied, "If in war, as in the choral competitions, he finds and produces the best men, he will most likely win in war as well. Besides, he is probably willing to spend more in winning a war for his state than in winning a choral competition for his tribe." *5*

"Do you mean, Socrates, that the same man may be a good choregus and a good general?" *6*

"I mean that when someone is a good executive, as long as he knows what he needs and how to get it, he may be a good executive of a chorus, an estate, the state, or the army."

"By Zeus," said Nichomachides, "I never thought that I would hear you say that good businessmen would be good generals!" *7*

"All right. Let's look at the duties of each of these and see if they are the same or different."

"By all means!"

"Isn't it the business of both to make their subordinates willing and obedient?" *8*

"Yes," agreed Nichomachides.

"And to assign to the right man each task to carry out?"

"This too."

"I think," continued Socrates, "both should punish evildoers and reward the good."

"Yes, indeed."

9   "Now what about good conduct toward their subordinates: Is this good for both businessman and general?"

"This too," agreed Nichomachides.

"Do you think it is important for both to find allies and aid, or not?" asked Socrates.

"Yes, I do think it is important for both."

"Should not both guard what they have?" asked Socrates.

"Absolutely!"

"Should both be painstaking and attentive to their duties?"

10   "Both alike should have all of these qualities. But fighting battles is not the concern of both," stated Nichomachides.

"Don't both have enemies?"

"Of course they do."

"Aren't both interested in winning over these enemies?"

11   "Certainly," replied Nichomachides, "but you are overlooking this problem: suppose it is necessary to fight. What good will it be to know how to run a business?"

"Surely the greatest help," replied Socrates. "For the good businessman knows that nothing is so profitable or pays so much as conquering one's enemies in battle, and that nothing is so unprofitable and entails such heavy loss as being defeated. So he will eagerly look for the means to victory and make his preparations. He will carefully note what dangers bring defeat, and avoid them. He will fight vigorously if he sees that his preparations assure victory, and what is just as important,

12   if he is unprepared, he will avoid going to battle. Do not look down on businessmen, Nichomachides. The difference between the management of private and of public affairs is merely a difference of size. In all other respects, the analogy holds; and what is most important, both involve dealing with men, and public and private transactions are carried out by the same, and not by different, men. The people in charge of public affairs employ the same men when they run their private business. Those who know how to use them succeed in both private and public affairs. Those who do not, fail in both."

Chapter 5: Conversation with the Younger Pericles on the Decline of Athens

Once when he was talking with Pericles, the son of the great   *1*
Pericles, Socrates said, "Now that you have become a general,[1]
Pericles, I hope that the state will be better off, win a better
reputation in war, and overcome its enemies."

"I should like what you say to come true, Socrates," Pericles
replied, "but I cannot see how this can come about."

Socrates said, "Do you want to discuss this and see how it is
possible even now?"

"Please!"

"Are you aware that the Athenians are not inferior in num-   *2*
bers to the Boeotians?" asked Socrates.

"Yes."

"Do you think that more good strong men could be selected
from among the Boeotians than from among the Athenians?"

"No. The Athenians are not at a disadvantage there."

"Who are the more closely united?"

"The Athenians, I think. For many of the Boeotians, who
have been exploited by the Thebans, feel much ill will against
them. I do not notice such a thing in Athens."

"Indeed, the Athenians are the most ambitious and the   *3*
kindest people of all—which is of no small importance in spur-
ring them on to run risks for their honor and their country."

"The Athenians," said Pericles, "need not fear criticism on
this score, either."

"Besides, no one has a greater heritage of great deeds in
the past than the Athenians. Many are encouraged by this inheritance to seek excellence and to become brave."

[1] Pericles, son of Aspasia and the great statesman, was one of the ten
generals involved in the battle of Arginusae (see note 8, page 7), after
which he returned to Athens for trial and was executed.

4   "All that you say is true, Socrates. Still, don't you see that ever since Tolmides' disaster with his thousands at Lebadeia [2] and Hippocrates' defeat at Delium,[3] our good reputation has decreased among the Boeotians, and the arrogance of the Thebans toward us has increased? As a result, the Boeotians, who formerly never dared, even on their own territory, to face the Athenians without the aid of the Lacedaimonians and the rest of the Peloponnesians, now threaten to invade Attica by themselves. On the other hand, the Athenians, who used to plunder Boeotia, now fear that the Boeotians will lay waste to Attica."

5   Socrates replied, "I am aware that this is the case. I think, however, that for a man who is a good leader, the state is now in a more favorable situation. For overconfidence brings neglect, rashness, and disobedience, while fear makes men

6   more careful and obedient, and better disciplined. As proof of this, look at the men now on the ships. When they aren't at all afraid, they are very disorderly. But let them fear a storm or the enemy, and they not only carry out all their orders, but they are even silent and eagerly await more orders, like dancers in a chorus."

7   Pericles replied, "If, however, they are especially obedient now, now is the time to say how we can arouse them to love again the virtue, fame, and prosperity of the old days."

8   "If," said Socrates, "we wanted them to collect money that others had, the best way to urge them to seize it would be to show them that it was their fathers' money, and really belonged to them. Since we wish them to strive to be first in virtue, we must then show them that it is their special inheritance from olden days, and that by striving for this they may become superior to all men."

9   "How," asked Pericles, "can we teach them this?"

"By reminding them, I think," replied Socrates, "that their

[2] Tolmides' defeat at Lebadeia occurred in 447 B.C. when Athens was attempting to extend her sphere of influence on the Greek mainland.

[3] In this battle near the small town of Delium in Boeotia (424 B.C.) Socrates fought.

earliest ancestors, of whom tradition tells, were really as great as they have heard."

"Do you refer to the judgment of the gods which Cecrops and his men pronounced because of their virtue?" [4]   *10*

"I mean also the birth and childhood of Erechtheus,[5] and the war he waged against the men from all the adjacent lands, and the war of the sons of Heracles against the inhabitants of the Peloponnese. I refer, also, to all the wars waged in Theseus' time, in all of which our ancestors proved clearly that they were better than their enemies. If you wish, I mean   *11* what their descendants did later, a little before our time: by themselves, they fought against the masters of all Asia and Europe as far as Macedonia, against men who possessed the greatest power and wealth the world had ever seen and who had performed the most daring deeds; and, what is more they and the Peloponnesians became first on land and on sea. These men also are said to have been much superior to their contemporaries." [6]

"So it is said," said Pericles.   *12*

"Therefore, although many migrations occurred in Greece, our ancestors remained in their own land; [7] many who were disputing rival claims entrusted their cases to our ancestors, and many who were oppressed by the more powerful took refuge with them."

Pericles said, "I wonder, Socrates, how our state declined   *13* so?"

Socrates replied, "For my part, I think that Athenians are like athletes who, because they can endure a lot and are strong, grow careless and lose to their opponents. Thus, be-

[4] Cecrops was the mythological king of Athens who judged the contest between Poseidon and Athena for the patronage of Athens. He chose Athena's gift of the olive tree instead of Poseidon's gift of a salt-water spring.

[5] Erechtheus is a mythological hero and king of Athens who waged war with the Thracians and Eleusinians.

[6] Socrates is referring to the Persian Wars and its heroes, such as Miltiades, Aristeides, and Themistocles.

[7] Athenians were very proud of their tradition of being autochthonous.

cause they were very superior, the Athenians became careless and therefore declined."

14   "Since this is the case," asked Pericles, "whatever could they do to recover their former virtue?"

Socrates said, "That doesn't seem to me to be anything mysterious. If they discover their ancestral customs and practice them just as their ancestors did, they will not become worse than their ancestors. Or if this fails, let them imitate the leaders of today and do the same things as their leaders. They will not become worse than their leaders by doing the same things. Indeed, if they are more careful, they will become even better."

15   Pericles said, "You mean that goodness and right are a long way away from our state. For when will the Athenians, like the Lacedaimonians, respect their elders? Now the Athenians begin by despising their parents, and go on to despise all their elders. When will they, like Spartans, train their bodies? Now they not only neglect their health, but even laugh at those who

16   try to keep physically fit. When will they obey their leaders? Now they delight in looking down on them! When will they unite with them? Instead of working with each other for their own benefit, they insult each other and feel more ill will toward each other than toward outsiders. Worst of all, both in their private associations and in public, they argue and bring as many suits against each other as possible. They prefer winning from each other to assisting each other. They treat public affairs as though they were someone else's concern, yet they fight about them and take special delight in having the power

17   to carry on these fights. Great ruin and evil have arisen in the state from this. The citizens envy and hate each other, so that I am in constant fear that some evil will come upon the state greater than it can endure."

18   Socrates replied, "Pericles, do not believe that the Athenians are sick with an incurable depravity. Don't you see how well disciplined the fleet is? How well they obey their managers in athletic contests and how they never fail to obey their trainers in the choruses?"

"It is very amazing," replied Pericles, "that such men obey 19
their leaders, while the hoplites and cavalry, who are reputed
to excel other citizens in true nobility, are the most disobedient of all!"

Socrates said, "Pericles, isn't the Areopagus made up of tried 20
and proven men?"

"Yes, indeed!"

"Do you know any men who are nobler, more law-abiding,
more revered, or more just in judging trials and in performing
all their other duties?"

"They aren't the people I am complaining about!"

"You must not then lose heart because you think that Athenians are not disciplined," said Socrates.

"But really," replied Pericles, "the army is where prudence, 21
discipline, and obedience are needed the most, and it has
none of these virtues!"

"Perhaps," replied Socrates, "the men who lead them don't
really know how to do so. Don't you see that no citharist,
chorus leader, or dance leader tries to lead unless he knows
how? The same is true of a wrestler or a pancratist. All who
are in charge of these must show where they learned their
skills. Most of the generals, on the other hand, are inexperienced. Nevertheless, I do not believe that you are like this, 22
but I think that you can say when you began to learn how
to be a general no less than you can say when you began to
learn to wrestle. You remember much from your father's experience as a general, and you have gathered you from every
source from which you could learn what is useful. You are
very anxious, I think, not to be unwittingly ignorant of what 23
is useful to a general; and if you see that you don't know
some such things, you will look for men who do know; you
will spare neither gifts nor favors in your efforts to have good
colleagues and to learn what you do not know."

"I realize, Socrates, that you do not say these things because 24
you think that I do this; rather, you are trying to teach me
that I should attend to all these problems, since I mean to be
a general. Indeed, I agree with you."

25   "Pericles, have you realized that great mountains lie around our country like a barrier against Boeotia? The passes through these are narrow and the interior is divided by very rugged mountains."

    "Certainly."

26   "Then you have heard that the Mysians and Pisidians within the territory of the Great King,[8] who have very strong positions and are lightly armed, are able to do much harm by invading the king's country, yet live free?"

    "Yes, I have heard this too."

27   "Don't you think that young Athenians, more lightly armed, and occupying the barricades formed by their country's mountains, would not only be more harmful to the enemy, but would also prove to be a strong bulwark for the citizens of their country?"

    "All your suggestions, Socrates," said Pericles, "are very useful, I think."

28   "If, then, they please you, sir, try them. What you accomplish with them will be fine for you and good for the state. If you fail, you will not hurt the state and you will not disgrace yourself."

Chapter 6: Advice to a Youthful Political Aspirant

1   Glaucon,[1] the son of Ariston, though he was not yet twenty years old, wanted to be a leader in the state and was trying to address the Assembly. None of his friends or relatives could stop him from being dragged from the podium and making himself ridiculous. Socrates, who was interested in Glaucon

8 The King of Persia.

1 Glaucon, Plato's brother. His family tree is:

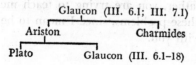

Glaucon (III. 6.1; III. 7.1)

Ariston   Charmides

Plato   Glaucon (III. 6.1–18)

through Glaucon's son Charmides and through Plato, was the only one who succeeded in stopping him. When he met Glaucon, he first contrived to get him to listen willingly by saying, "Glaucon, have you decided to be a leader in our state?"

"I have, O Socrates."

"By Zeus, of all the things among mankind, that is fine! Clearly, if you succeed in holding office, you will have the power to get what you wish and you will be able to help your friends. You will elevate your father's household, increase your fatherland, and be famed—first in the state, then in Greece, and perhaps, like Themistocles, even among the barbarians.[2] Wherever you may be, you will be admired by all."

When Glaucon heard this, he was proud and gladly lingered. Then Socrates added, "Isn't it clear that if you want to receive honor, you must benefit the state?"

"Absolutely."

"By the gods," exclaimed Socrates, "Don't keep it back from us! Tell us how you will begin to help the state!"

When Glaucon was silent as if thinking then for the first time how he would begin, Socrates said, "If you wanted to increase the estate of a friend, you would try to make him richer. Would you try then to make the state richer?"

"Absolutely."

"Would the state be richer if it received more revenue?"

"Quite likely."

"Then tell us the sources of revenue for the state now, and how much they yield. For you must have studied the problem so that you can make up the difference if the income falls below what is anticipated and so that you can find new sources of revenue when the old ones lapse."

"But, by Zeus," said Glaucon, "I have not yet studied this."

"If you have omitted this, tell us what the expenses of the state are. Clearly you intend to cut out excessive expenditures."

"But, by Zeus, I have not yet studied this."

2 Themistocles fled from Athens to Persia where King Artaxerxes I gave him the cities of Magnesia on the Meander, Myrus, Lampsacus, and part of the Troad.

"Then," said Socrates, "we will postpone enriching the state. For how can you pay attention to this unless you know the income and expenses?"

7 "But Socrates," said Glaucon, "it is possible to enrich the state at the expense of its enemies."

"By Zeus, yes—if the state is stronger. If it proves to be weaker than the enemy, the state would only be throwing away its wealth."

"You are right."

8 "Therefore, in order for man to give advice about whom to attack, the strength of both the state and of the enemy must be known. This way, if the state has greater power, he may advise them to try war; otherwise he may persuade them to be cautious."

9 "Correct."

"First tell us the naval and land power of our state, then of the enemy."

"But, by Zeus, I can't tell you this offhand."

"If you have made notes, bring what you have written, and I shall be glad to hear it."

"But, by Zeus," cried Glaucon, "I haven't even made notes on the subject."

10 "So," said Socrates, "we shall refrain from advising war, at least at first. For having just entered office, you have perhaps not yet had time to make this study because of the size of the forces. But I am sure that you have already concerned yourself with the country's defenses, and that you know how many garrisons are well located and how many are not, and how many fortresses operate efficiently and how many do not. You will propose to improve the well-located garrisons and you will do away with the unnecessary ones."

11 "By Zeus," said Glaucon, "I would do away with them all! Their guarding amounts to stealing from the country!"

"But, if you did away with the garrisons," replied Socrates, "don't you think that anyone who wanted to do so would have the power to plunder? Still, you must previously have gone in person and found this out? Or else, how do you know that the garrisons do a poor job?"

"I surmise it."

"Shouldn't we give advice when we no longer surmise something, but actually know it?"

"Perhaps," said Glaucon, "that is better."

"Now for the question of the silver mines: I know that you have not yet visited them so as to be able to tell why they now produce less than before."

"I have not been there."

"By Zeus," said Socrates, "The district [3] is said to be very unhealthful; thus when you are called upon for advice, that will be excuse enough for you."

"You are making fun of me," said Glaucon.

"I know that you have not neglected this problem: how long will the grain supply last the state, and how much is needed annually? You must know this so that when the state needs food, you, from your knowledge, can give advice to the state about these necessities, and can help and even save the state."

Glaucon replied, "What you describe is an enormous task if I shall have to study such things."

"Nevertheless," said Socrates, "a man cannot manage his estate well unless he knows what is needed and sees to it that these needs are all supplied. But since the state consists of more than ten thousand homes, and it is difficult to take care of so many homes at once, how is it that you have not tried to increase even one household—that of your uncle—first? For he needs help. If you can do this you can do even more. If you cannot be useful to one man, how could you help many? A man who cannot carry the weight of one talent obviously should not try to carry more, should he?"

"But I would help my uncle's estate, if only he would listen to me," said Glaucon.

"Then," said Socrates, "how do you think you would make

[3] Laurium, south of Athens in Attica.

16 all the Athenians listen to you (and your uncle among them!) if you cannot make even your uncle listen? Be careful, Glaucon! While you desire a fine reputation, you might get just the opposite! Don't you see how dangerous it is to say or do what you do not understand? Remember all the people you know like this, whom you have seen say and do things about which they know nothing. Do you think they get praise for such deeds instead of blame, or are admired instead of despised?

17 Consider, too, those who do understand what they say and what they do; you will find, I believe, that in every kind of undertaking, the men who are most esteemed and admired come from among those who know the most, while the men who are of ill repute and are despised come from among the

18 most ignorant. If, therefore, you wish to be honored and admired in the state, try to bring it about that you really understand what you want to do. If you excel others in this and then put your hand to affairs of state, I would not be surprised if you easily achieved what you wish."

Chapter 7: Advice to a Distinguished Citizen

1 Socrates observed that Charmides,[1] the son of Glaucon, was a remarkable man with much more ability than the men involved in politics at the time. Yet Charmides refused to go to the Assembly or to take an interest in the affairs of state. Socrates said, "Tell me, Charmides, suppose a man is able to win the wreath of victory in a contest, to gain honor for this, and to make his state more famed throughout Greece, and yet is not willing to enter these contests. What would you think of him?

"Obviously, I would consider him weak and cowardly!"

2 "Suppose," said Socrates, "that a man was able, by con-

[1] The uncle of Plato; see note I, p. 80.

cerning himself in his country's affairs, to do good for the
state and thus win honor. If he avoids doing this, wouldn't it
be reasonable to consider him cowardly?"

"Maybe. Why ask me this?"

"Because I think that you have the ability to enter politics,
yet you avoid concerning yourself, or taking the part that you,
as a citizen, should take in the state."

Charmides said, "Where have you ever observed and learned   3
of these abilities of mine?"

"In your associations with the men engaged in affairs of
state. When they consult you, I see that you give good advice.
When they make a mistake, I see that you give sound criticism."

"Socrates," he replied, "it is not the same thing to argue in   4
private and to debate before the people!"

"But," said Socrates, "the man who is able to count can do
so in public as well as by himself. Men who play the cithara
best by themselves also win in public contests."

"Don't you see," said Charmides, "that shame and fear are   5
natural to men, and occur much more before crowds than in
private conversations?"

"I have been eager to teach you a lesson. In front of the
wisest men you feel no shame and before the most powerful
people you have no fear, yet you feel ashamed to speak before
the most stupid and weak! Do the cleaners, shoemakers, car-   6
penters, blacksmiths, farmers, merchants, or those who make
exchanges in the marketplace and worry about buying something cheap so as to sell it at a profit, do these make you feel
shame? These are the men who make up the Assembly. You   7
are no different from a professional who fears an amateur!
You are at ease in discussions with the leaders of the state—
some of whom look down upon you—and you are much better
than the men who concern themselves with debate before the
state. Despite this, simply because you are afraid of being
laughed at, you avoid speaking with men who have never
given a thought to politics and who do not look down on
you."

8   "What! Haven't you often seen men in the Assembly laugh
at people who say the right thing?" said Charmides.

"Yes, and I have seen the others do so also. I am amazed at
you! When the politicians laugh at you, you are easily able to
master them, but you think you cannot deal at all with the
9   Assembly! My dear sir, don't be ignorant of yourself! Don't
make the same mistake that most people make. The Assembly
swears to look out for the affairs of others and is not fit to
examine itself. Do not avoid your duty! Try rather to pay
some heed to yourself. Do not neglect the state if you can improve the state. For if affairs of state go well, not only will the
other citizens profit, but so will your friends, and, not the
least, you yourself."

Chapter 8: On the Good and the Beautiful

1   When Aristippus tried to cross-examine Socrates as Socrates
had previously cross-examined him, Socrates wanted his
friends to profit; so, unlike those who are on guard as to
whether or not an argument is distorted, he answered like a
2   man who is determined to do what is right. First Aristippus
asked Socrates if he knew anything good—this was so that he
might demonstrate that a good thing was sometimes also bad,
should Socrates name something like food, drink, money,
health, strength, or daring. Realizing that if we have a troublesome problem, we want the solution, Socrates replied with the
3   answer that would do the most good: "Are you asking me if I
know of something good for a fever?"

"No!"

"For eye trouble?"

"Not for that either."

"Something good for hunger?"

"No, not for hunger!"

"But if you ask me if I know something good that is good
for nothing, I don't know. And I don't need to know."

Again Aristippus asked Socrates if he knew something beautiful and Socrates replied, "Yes, many things." 4

"Are they all alike?" asked Aristippus.

"Some as dissimilar as can be."

"How can that which is unlike the beautiful be beautiful?"

"Because, by Zeus," replied Socrates, "it is possible for a man who is a beautiful racer to be very different from another who is a beautiful wrestler. The shield, which is a beautiful defense, is very unlike the javelin, which is beautiful for easy, swift throwing."

"But your reply is no different from the one which you 5 made when I asked you if you knew something good."

"Do you think that the good is one thing and the beautiful another? Don't you know that all things are beautiful and good in relation to the same standard? First of all, virtue is not good in relation to one thing, and beautiful in relation to another. Secondly, men are called good and beautiful in the same way and in relation to the same standard. Human bodies appear beautiful and good in relation to the same standard. Everything that men use is thought to be good and beautiful in relation to the thing for which it is useful."

"But is a dung-basket beautiful?" 6

"Yes, by Zeus," replied Socrates, "and a golden shield is ugly—if the dung-basket is well made for its purpose, and the golden shield is poorly made."

"Do you mean," asked Aristippus, "that the same things are both beautiful and ugly?"

"Yes, by Zeus, and both good and bad. For frequently some- 7 thing good for hunger is bad for a fever, and what is good for a fever is bad for hunger. Frequently what is beautiful racing form is ugly wrestling form, and what is beautiful wrestling form is ugly racing form. Everything is good and beautiful according to how well it serves its purpose, and everything is bad and ugly according to how poorly it serves its purpose."

By saying that the same house must be at once beautiful 8 and useful, he taught, I think, what sort of houses should be built. His argument went like this: "When a man plans to

9 have the sort of house he should have, shouldn't he design it to be both as pleasant and as useful as possible?" When this was admitted, he continued, "Is it not pleasant to have the house cool in the summer and warm in the winter?" When they agreed to this as well, he said, "When houses face south, in the winter the sun lights the inner room and in the summer makes shade because its path is directly over us and the roof. If, then, it is good to have the house this way, we must build the southern side higher, so that the winter sun is not blocked out. The north side must be lower, so that the cold winds

10 don't blow in. To put it briefly, the house in which a man finds the most pleasant shelter at all seasons and which can keep his possessions safest is the house that is presumably the most pleasant and the most beautiful. Painting and decorations deprive us of more comfort than they offer."

For temples and altars he said that the most suitable site was one that was the most conspicuous and solitary, since it is pleasant to pray when we catch sight of them, and pleasant to approach them when we feel holy.

Chapter 9: On Courage, Wisdom, Madness, Envy, Leisure, Rulers, Good Conduct

1   At another time, Socrates was asked whether courage was acquired by learning or was natural. He replied, "I think that in the face of dangers one soul naturally becomes stronger than another, just as one body grows stronger than another when faced with hard work. I observe, moreover, that men brought up under the same laws and customs vary widely in

2 the amount of daring they may have. Yet I do believe that any nature can develop more courage through learning and practice. Quite obviously, Scythians and Thracians would not dare to take up heavy shields and spears to do battle with the Spartans. And quite plainly the Spartans would be unwilling to fight Thracians with light shields and javelins or the Scyth-

3 ians with bows. Similarly, in all sorts of other ways, I observe,

men naturally differ from each other, yet all improve with practice. So it is clear that every man, whether talented or stupid by nature, must learn and practice the pursuits in which he wants to win a good reputation."

Socrates made no distinction between wisdom [*sophia*] and temperance [*sophrosýne*]. When a man recognized what was good and what was beautiful, and behaved accordingly, and when he knew what was ugly and avoided it, Socrates judged him both wise and temperate. He was asked if he thought that the men who knew what they ought to do, yet did the opposite, were both wise and unrestrained.

"No! Instead they are unwise and unrestrained. I think all men choose, from among the possibilities, to do what they think will be of the greatest advantage to themselves. Men, I believe, who do not act rightly are neither wise nor temperate." He also said that justice, as well as every other kind of virtue, was wisdom. "For just acts and all the acts performed virtuously are good and beautiful. The men who know what is good and what is beautiful will never choose anything else; but those who do not know, cannot do what is good or beautiful, and even if they try, they fail. The wise, therefore, can do what is good and beautiful; the unwise cannot, and they only fail if they try. Since just acts and other good and beautiful acts are all virtuous actions, clearly justice, as well as every other virtue, is wisdom."

Madness [*mania*], he claimed, was the opposite of wisdom. Nevertheless, he did not think that madness was ignorance [*anepistemosýne*]. He thought that the closest thing to madness was not to know yourself and to think and assume that you know what you do not know. People do not consider anyone mad who makes mistakes in things most people do not know anyway; rather, a man is called mad if he is mistaken about things most people know. Suppose, for example, a man thinks he is so tall that he must stoop when he goes through the gates of the city wall. Or suppose he thinks he is so strong that he can lift houses, or tries something else everyone knows is impossible. This is madness. People do not think that those who make small mistakes are mad, but just as they call strong desire "love," so they call great senselessness "madness."

8   In his study of envy, he found that it was a kind of grief, but not grief at a friend's misfortunes or an enemy's successes. He said that only the men who are distressed at their friends' successes feel envy. When several expressed amazement that anyone would grieve at a friend's success, he reminded them that many people were like this and, though they cannot neglect their friends in the time of trouble and they even help them in their misfortunes, they are grieved when their friends are fortunate. Sensible men do not feel this, but fools always do.

9   He examined the nature of leisure and said he found most men were doing something, whatever it might be. Gamblers and clowns do something, yet all these are idle, for they could go and do something better. No one is at leisure to go from better activities to worse. If he should do so, since he has not leisure, he is doing evil.

10   He said that kings and archons were not those who held the scepter, were elected by the electorate or chosen by lot, or gained power by force or treachery; rather, they were those
11   who knew how to rule. Whenever someone would agree that the duty of a ruler is to give orders and that the duty of a subject is to obey, he used to prove that on a ship, the one who knows is the one who rules, while the owner and all the rest on board obey the man who knows. In farming, in sickness, and in sports, landowners, patients, and men in training (as well as all the rest who are in something that demands care) do the work themselves, if they think they know how. Otherwise they obey men who do know, if such men are nearby. If the experts are not nearby, they send for them, so that they can obey them and do what they ought to do. Socrates used to point out that women rule men when it comes to spinning
12   wool, for women know how to spin and men do not. When the reply was made to this that a tyrant could refuse to obey good counselors, Socrates used to ask, "How could he refuse to obey when there is a penalty imposed on the man who dis-

regards good counsel? For if a man disregards good counsel in some matters he will surely make a mistake; and when he makes a mistake he will be punished." To the man who said that a tyrant could put a loyal subject to death, Socrates replied, "Do you think that a tyrant suffers no loss when he puts his strongest allies to death? Do you think he suffers merely a chance loss? Do you imagine that by doing this he is saving himself, and not just swiftly destroying himself?"

Once a man asked Socrates what he thought was the best practice for a man to follow. Socrates replied, "Good conduct [*eupraxia*]." When asked another time if he thought good luck [*eutychia*] was a practice, he answered, "Luck and conduct are complete opposites, I believe. The reason is this: suppose a man who does not seek to get something he needs, does get it. This is good luck, I think. Suppose a man learns and studies how to do well. This, I believe, is good conduct, and I believe that men who practice this do well. The best men and those dearest to the gods are the men who conduct themselves well, whether in farming, medicine, or politics. A man who does not conduct himself well is not useful, nor is he dear to the gods."

Chapter 10: Advice to Artists

But besides this, even when Socrates talked with professional artists, he was useful to them. Once he went to see Parrhasius the painter and said to him, "Parrhasius, is painting a representation of visible objects? Through colors you represent and closely imitate bodies that are old or young, smooth or rough, soft or hard, light or dark, high or low."

"That is right," he answered.

"When you portray beautiful forms, since it is not easy for one man to be completely flawless, you unite the best features of many men, so that you make the whole body appear beautiful."

"Yes, we do that."

3   "How do you represent the state of mind [*ethos tes psyches*] that is the most winning, the most agreeable, the most friendly, the most desirable, and the most lovable? Or can't this be imitated?"

"How, Socrates, could I represent what has no measure, no color, none of the qualities which you just mentioned, and is completely invisible?"

4   "Doesn't it happen that a man looks at people in a friendly or hostile way?"

"I think so," replied Parrhasius.

"Can't this be imitated in the eyes?"

"Yes, indeed."

"When good or evil befalls friends, do you think that men who are concerned over this have the same expression on their faces as do those who are not concerned?"

"By Zeus, surely not! For they are radiant because of the good or crestfallen because of the evil that has befallen their friends."

"Therefore, it is possible to represent this," said Socrates.

"Yes, indeed," was the reply.

5   "But really, magnificence and freedom, lowliness and slavery, temperance and prudence, insolence and vulgarity, are apparent in the face and bearing of a man, whether he stands still or is in motion."

"You are right," said Parrhasius.

"Therefore, even these things can be represented."

"Yes, indeed."

"Do you find it more pleasant to look at men whose characters appear beautiful, good, and lovable, or at men whose characters appear ugly, evil, and hateful?"

"By Zeus, there is a great difference, Socrates."

6   Once Socrates came to the house of the sculptor Cleiton and was talking with him. "Cleiton, I see and I know that you make beautiful runners, wrestlers, boxers, and pancratists. The most attractive thing to men's eyes is the appearance of real life in your statues. How do you get this effect? "

7   Cleiton, at a loss, did not answer at once.

"Is it by actually representing the forms of the living that you make your statues appear more lifelike? "

"Yes," replied Cleiton.

"When you represent the parts of the body as drawn up or down by the pose, or contracted or outstretched, or held taut or relaxed, don't you make your statues appear more lifelike and convincing? "

"Quite so," said Cleiton.

"Doesn't the imitation of the emotions of these bodies in action bring some pleasure to the spectator? "   8

"That is likely," replied Cleiton.

"Shouldn't you then represent the menacing eyes of fighters and the triumphant expression of the winners? "

"Certainly."

"Then," said Socrates, "the sculptor must represent the activities of the soul through form."

Socrates visited Pistias the armor-maker, who proceeded to   9
show him some well-made breastplates. Socrates exclaimed, "By Hera, that is a beautiful invention! The breastplate covers the parts that need protection but does not interfere with the use of the arms! But tell me, Pistias, why do you charge more   10
for your breastplates, when you do not make them stronger or of costlier material than the others? "

"Because, Socrates, I make better-proportioned breastplates."

"When you set a higher price, do you prove the superiority of the proportions by their measure, or by their weight? For I imagine that you do not make them all equal and alike if you make them fit."

"But by Zeus, I make them fit! A breastplate is useless without that! "

"But," said Socrates, "aren't some human bodies well pro-   11
portioned and others badly proportioned? "

"Of course! "

"How do you, then, make a well proportioned breastplate fit a badly proportioned body? "

"By fitting it. If it fits, it is well proportioned."

"I think you mean that it is not well-proportioned in itself,   12 but in relation to the wearer. In the same way you would say that a shield or a chlamys that fits is well proportioned. The other things also are likely to be this way, according to your

13   argument. Perhaps there is another advantage, and not a small one, to a good fit."

"Tell me, Socrates, if you know."

"The well-fitting breastplates crush you less with their weight than the poorly fitted ones, although their weight is the same. For the poorly fitted breastplates hang all their weight from the shoulders or press on some other part of the body, and so become hard to wear and uncomfortable. The well-fitting breastplates, on the other hand, are almost more like accessories than burdens, because their weight is distributed over the collarbone, shoulder blades, shoulders, chest, back, and stomach."

14   "You have given the very reason that I think my products are worth the most. Yet some people prefer to buy ornamented and gold-plated breastplates."

"If in consequence," said Socrates, "they buy a piece that fits poorly, I think they are making a poor buy, even though it is

15   ornamented and gold-plated! How can breastplates fit exactly when the body is never still, but sometimes is bent over and sometimes erect?"

"They can't."

"Do you mean," asked Socrates, "that a good fit is not the exact fit, but the fit that does not bother the wearer?"

"You yourself have said it, Socrates, and you are absolutely right."

Chapter 11: A Conversation with the Courtesan Theodote

1   Once there was in Athens a beautiful woman whose name was Theodote—the sort of woman who went to anyone who prevailed upon her. One of the bystanders mentioned her and

said that the beauty of the woman defied words. Painters, he
added, went to her to paint her and to them she showed as much
of her beauty as was fitting. Socrates cried, "We must go see for
ourselves! If her beauty defies words, we can't learn of it by
hearsay! "

The bystander who had spoken said, "You're there already!
Follow me." So they came to Theodote's house and watched   2
her posing before a painter whom they found there. After the
painter had stopped, Socrates said, "Men, should we thank
Theodote for showing us her beauty or should she thank us
for looking at it? If the display is more profitable to her,
shouldn't she thank us? If it is more profitable to us, shouldn't
we thank her? "

Someone said that he was right, so Socrates proceeded, "She   3
has already won praise from us and when we spread the news
further, she will profit still more. Already we long to touch
what we've seen; we shall go away excited, and we shall long
for her when we are gone. As a result, we shall become her
slaves and she our mistress."

"By Zeus," said Theodote, "If this is so, I owe you thanks
for looking."

Then Socrates saw that she was luxuriously dressed and   4
that her mother, who was with her, had fine clothes and
jewels. She had also many servants who were good-looking and
well cared for, and her house was lavishly furnished in all
other respects. "Tell me, Theodote," he said, "do you have
a farm? "

"No! "

"But do you have a house that brings in an income? "

"I do not! "

"Surely you own some skilled workers? "

"Not even skilled workers," she replied.

"Then where do you get your income? "

"My livelihood comes from friends I pick up who want to
help me."

"By Hera, a fine source of income, Theodote. It is much   5
better to have friends than sheep, goats, or cattle! Do you

trust to luck and wait for a friend to settle upon you like a fly, or have you devised a method?"

6   "How could I devise a method for this?" she asked.

"By Zeus, more becomingly than spiders! For you know how spiders hunt for their living. They weave fine webs and feed on anything that happens to fall into them."

7   "Do you advise me to make some kind of a trap?"

"Yes, for you should not think that you can hunt friends, the most valuable game of all, without any art! Don't you see that hunters use many tricks to catch even rabbits, which are game of little value? Because rabbits come out to feed at night, they have dogs trained to hunt at night and they hunt

8   with these. Because rabbits disappear at daybreak, the hunters use dogs that track them by scent from their feeding place to their holes. Then because rabbits are very fast and can escape by running in the open, they have other swift dogs which are ready to catch the rabbits on foot. And because some escape even these dogs, they put up nets at the paths where they escape, so as to catch them when they fall into the nets."

9   "With what sort of thing should I hunt friends?"

"By Zeus, instead of dogs, get someone who will track down and find rich good friends, and who, once they are found, will contrive to ensnare them in your nets."

10   "What kind of nets do I have?" said Theodote.

"One, surely, which is especially all-embracing—your body! In the body is a soul with which you have learned to please with a glance, and to say what delights; to receive gracefully the suitor who cares, and to get rid of the voluptuary; to be thoughtful enough to visit a friend when he is sick, and to congratulate him on his successes; and, if he cares for you a great deal, to gratify him with your whole soul. I well know that you know how to make love gently and affectionately and that your friends satisfy you. I am sure also that you win them over by deed, not by word."

"By Zeus," cried Theodote, "I use none of these techniques."

11   "Yet," said Socrates, "it makes a great difference to behave

naturally and correctly toward a man. For you do not catch and hold a friend by force. It is by being kind and pleasing that the game is captured and held faithful."

"You are right, Socrates."

"You must first ask your suitors for things which will be the least bother to give. Then return their favors in kind. This is the way they will become your best friends, will remain your friends for the longest time, and will help you the most. You will give them the most gratification if you wait to give favors until they ask. You see that the best food, when served before it is wanted, appears distasteful and absolutely nauseating if served to a person who has already eaten his fill. Even poor food is good to someone starving."

"How can I make men starved for my fare?"

"By Zeus, first of all, by not offering it to them when they have already been satisfied, and by not suggesting anything until they no longer have plenty and again feel a need. Secondly, when they feel the need, remind them by the most decorous behavior possible, by seeming unwilling to yield, and by being reluctant until they feel the sharpest possible need. At such a time the same favors are much different from those given before there is a desire for them."

Theodote said, "Why then, Socrates, haven't you become my companion in the hunt for friends?"

"By Zeus, if you convince me!"

"How can I convince you?"

"If you need me," said Socrates, "you will seek and find the way yourself."

"Come and see me often," said Theodote.

Socrates, making fun of his own freedom from employment, replied, "Theodote, it is not very easy for me to find leisure time. Many private and public affairs keep me busy. I have many women who won't let me leave day or night, and these are learning charms and magic spells from me."

"Do you understand charms and magic spells too?"

"Why is it, do you think, that Apollodorus and Antisthenes, here, never leave my side? Why have Cebes and Simmias come from Thebes? You can be sure that these things do not happen without many charms, spells, and magic wheels."

18   "Let me use your wheel," said Theodote, "so that I can turn it for you first of all."

"But by Zeus, I don't want to be attracted to you. I want you to come to me! "

"I'll come," she replied, "Only be sure you receive me!"

"I shall receive you, unless some woman more lovable than you is inside with me."

Chapter 12: On Keeping Physically Fit

1   Socrates saw that one of his companions, Epigenes, was in poor physical condition though he was young, and said, "You are as badly out of condition, Epigenes, as an amateur."

"Socrates, I am an amateur! "

"No more than the men who intend to be Olympic contestants! Do you think the life-and-death struggle against the enemy that the Athenians are perhaps going to enter upon is

2   insignificant? It isn't only that a few die in battle, or else save themselves disgracefully, because their bodies are out of condition. Many people are captured alive for this reason, and either spend the rest of their lives in the cruelest slavery, if it is so fated, or, after falling into the worst straits and sometimes paying a ransom greater than they possess, spend the rest of their lives wretched and destitute of the barest necessities. Many people get disgraceful reputations and are con-

3   sidered cowards because of their bodily weakness. Do you scorn these "rewards" for weakness, and think that you can bear such suffering easily? I really think that it is much easier and pleasanter to endure the pains of keeping one's body in condition. Is it that you think it is healthier and, in other ways, more useful to have the body out of condition than to have it in good condition? Or do you look down on the effects

4   of being in good physical condition? Indeed, everything that happens to the healthy body is quite the opposite of what

happens to the sickly body. Men whose bodies are in good condition are healthy and strong. Consequently many save themselves creditably from the enemy, and escape all sorts of dreadful things, while many others aid their friends and do good for their fatherland. Therefore, they win gratitude, earn fine reputations, and achieve the highest honors, thus spending the rest of their lives better and more pleasantly, and leaving their children a better start in life. That the state does 5 not have public military training is no reason for a man to neglect it as a private citizen. Instead he should attend to it himself. You know that in any contest or business you are not worse off because your body is in better condition. In everything man does, his body is useful. In every function of the body, it is important for the body to be in the best condition possible. Even in what seems to entail the least use of the 6 body—thinking—who does not know that many errors are made because the body is not healthy? Loss of memory, depression, discontent, even madness, frequently attack the minds of many whose bodies are in ill health, so that they forget all they once knew. Those whose bodies are in good condition 7 have good protection and there is no risk of undergoing the sufferings caused by ill health. Quite the contrary! Being in good physical condition is likely to produce the results that are the exact opposite of those of being in poor physical condition. What would a sane man not endure to obtain the opposite effects to those I have mentioned? It is, besides, shame- 8 ful for a man to grow old through neglect, before he sees what kind of a man he may be when his body is in the finest and strongest condition. He can never find this out if he neglects his body, for he cannot wish to become this automatically."

Chapter 13: Socrates Plays the Gadfly

Once a man was angry because he said "Hello" and got no 1 answer. "Ridiculous!" said Socrates. "You would not have become angry if you had met a man in worse health than you. Yet when you meet a man who is in a worse temper, you are angry."

2   Another man said that eating was unpleasant. "Acumenus [1] has a good cure for that," replied Socrates.

"What? "

"Stop eating and you will then lead a pleasanter, cheaper, and healthier life."

3   When, moreover, another man said that the drinking water at his home was hot, Socrates remarked, "Then your water will be all ready for you when you want to take a warm bath! "

"But it is too cold to wash in! "

"Do your slaves complain when they drink it or wash in it? "

"By Zeus, no! I have often wondered at how content they are to use it for either purpose."

Socrates asked, "Where is the water warmer to drink, in your house or in the Asclepieion? " [2]

"In the Asclepieion," he replied.

"And where is the water cooler to bathe in? In your house or at the Amphiareion? " [3]

"In the Amphiareion."

"Consider then that you are probably more difficult to please than slaves or invalids."

4   A man punished his attendant severely and Socrates asked why he was angry at his slave. "Because," he replied, "he is a glutton and a fool! He is greedy for money and lazy."

"Have you ever thought who needs more lashes, you or your slave? "

5   A man was afraid of the road to Olympia and Socrates asked, "Why do you dread the journey? When you are at home aren't you on your feet most of the day? While you are

[1] A doctor whose son, Eryximachus, Plato mentions frequently among the companions of Socrates.

[2] There was a shrine to Asclepius in Athens on the south slope of the Acropolis.

[3] The shrine of the hero Amphiareus is in Attica.

journeying to Olympia you will walk before breakfast; then you will walk and eat dinner and rest. Don't you realize that if you put together all the walks you take in five or six days you will easily walk from Athens to Olympia? It is more pleasant to set out a day early than a day late, for to be forced to lengthen the distance to be covered in a day is difficult, while to journey an extra day allows some leisure. It is better to hurry to set out than to hurry on the journey."

When another man said that he was almost dead after a   *6*
long journey, Socrates asked him if he was carrying a load.

"By Zeus, not I! Just my cloak."

"Did you travel alone, or did you have an attendant?" asked Socrates.

"I had an attendant."

"Was he loaded down or empty-handed? "

"By Zeus, he carried the covers and other equipment."

"How did he fare from the journey? " continued Socrates.

"Better than I, it seems! "

"Suppose you had to carry his load? How do you think you would feel? "

"Terrible, by Zeus! I could not have carried it."

"Do you think, by any chance, that a man can be called trained if he is not able to do as much work as a slave?"

Chapter 14: On Table Manners

Whenever some of those who met together to eat brought   *1*
very little food to go with their bread and others brought a lot, Socrates told the slave to serve the small amount in the center for all alike, or to divide it equally among everyone. Then those who brought a lot were ashamed to take a share in what was put out for all without adding their own. And so they also added theirs to the rest. Since they got no more than those who brought a small amount of food to go with their bread, they ceased to buy expensive food.

2   Socrates observed once that one of the diners stopped eating bread and ate the other food alone; apropos of the conversation, which was about the meaning of words, he said, "Men, we must say what is meant when a man is called a glutton. Everyone eats food with his bread when there is some, yet somehow I think that men are not called gluttons for this

3   action. If someone eats his food without bread (and he is not in training, but does it for pleasure) do you think he seems to be a glutton or not?"

"It is hard to say who else would be called a glutton!" was the reply.

One of those present said, "Isn't a man a glutton if he eats a lot of food with only a little bit of bread?"

Socrates answered, "I think he could be called a glutton quite justly. And when men pray to the gods for a good harvest of wheat, they probably pray for a good harvest of

4   food other than bread." When Socrates had said this, one young man, thinking that these words were aimed at him, did not stop eating the food, but simply took more bread. Socrates noticed this and said, "Watch, you who are sitting near him, to see if he is eating bread with some food or food with a bit of bread."

5   Once Socrates observed someone else eating many different foods with one serving of bread. "Can you imagine a spread more extravagant or ruinous than the one a man eats when he puts all kinds of seasoned sauces into his mouth at once? By mixing up more than the cooks mixed, he makes it more extravagant! He mixes what the cooks will not mix, because they consider the mixtures unsuitable. If the cooks are right,

6   he is wrong and is ruining their art. Yet how ridiculous it is for a man to obtain the most knowledgeable cooks, and then to set aside what they have made when he himself doesn't even claim to know their art at all! Something else also happens to the man who eats many things together: when many foods are not served he misses his usual variety; while the man who is used to one dish with one serving of bread doesn't

mind at all eating only one dish when a variety is not provided.

Socrates used to say that in Attic dialect, the term "to dine well" meant simply "to eat," and that the term "well" in the phrase "to dine well" meant that which did no harm to the body or soul. Thus did Socrates apply the phrase "to dine well" to the men who live temperately.

7

BOOK FOUR

SOCRATES, BENEFACTOR AND EDUCATOR OF THE ATHENIANS

Chapter 1: How Socrates Helped People

1 Socrates was so useful in every circumstance and in every way that to even an ordinarily perceptive observer it was apparent that nothing was more useful than to be with Socrates and to spend time with him, no matter what the circumstances, or where. Even when they were not with Socrates and simply remembered him, the men who followed him and were used to being with him derived no small benefit. For in his lighter moments, no less than in his serious ones, Socrates

2 profited those with whom he spent time. Often he said, "I love so and so." Clearly, however, the men he desired were not those whose bodies were well endowed with beauty, but those whose souls were well endowed with virtue. He judged natures good on the basis of the fact that they learned quickly whatever he called to their attention, and that they remembered what they learned, and that they desired all the various lessons by which they could manage home and state, and could deal completely capably with men and their affairs. He believed that men educated like this not only could be happy themselves and manage their homes well, but also could make other

3 men and their states happy. He did not approach everybody in the same way. When men thought that nature had made them good and therefore scorned his teaching, he used to teach that the natures which seemed the most talented were those that most needed education. He pointed out how among horses those of the finest breeding, which are the most spirited and mettlesome, become the most useful and the best horses

if they are broken in as colts; and if they are not broken in, they are intractable and very poor. As for the dogs of the finest breeding, who have endurance and are aggressive in the face of wild beasts, those that are well trained become the best and the most useful in hunting while the untrained dogs are good for nothing, wild, and very disobedient. It is the same *4* thing with men of the finest breeding, that is to say the bravest in soul and the best able to carry out what they undertake. If they are educated and learn what they must do, they become the best and most useful, and they do the greatest and the most good. The uneducated and untaught become the most evil and harmful, for they do not know how to judge what they should do. They often take part in evil undertakings and, because they are high-spirited and energetic, they are very hard to restrain and very stubborn; therefore they do the greatest evil. Some men were conceited because of their *5* wealth and thought that they did not need an education. They considered that wealth was all they needed for doing what they wanted and for obtaining honor among their fellow men. Socrates taught these men by remarking, "A man is a fool if he thinks that he can discriminate between harmful and useful things without having learned how to do so. He is also a fool if he thinks that he will do what is profitable merely by supplying what he wants from his wealth, without having discriminated between what is harmful and useful. He is senseless if he thinks that he is doing well and has been well enough prepared for making a living without being able to do what is profitable. He is also senseless if he thinks that on account of wealth, he will, without knowing anything, be thought good in something or will have a good reputation, when he is considered good for nothing."

Chapter 2: Socrates Educates Euthydemus

I shall now describe how he treated the men who believed *1* that they had the finest education and who were conceited because of their wisdom. He saw that Euthydemus "the Hand-some" collected many of the writings of the highly esteemed poets and sophists; as a result, he already thought that he was superior to his contemporaries in wisdom, and he had great hopes that he would excel all others in his ability to speak and to get things done. Socrates first saw him when he was not yet coming to the agora because of his youth, but when he wanted to discuss something, he sat at one of the saddler's shops near the agora. Accordingly, Socrates himself went there with some of his companions. First someone asked whether it was because of his innate ability, or because of his companion-ship with a wise man, that Themistocles excelled his fellow citizens so much that the state looked to him whenever they needed a capable man. Socrates, wishing to arouse Euthy-demus, said that if men could not excel in the minor arts and crafts without teachers, it was simple-minded to think that the governing of a state, the greatest of all works, came auto-matically to men. Once when Euthydemus was again present, Socrates saw that he withdrew from the group and took care not to seem to admire Socrates for his wisdom. "Men," said Socrates, "when Euthydemus, here, comes of age and the state offers him an opportunity to speak on a measure, he will not withdraw from the council. This is obvious from the way he proceeds now. I think that he has prepared a fine introduc-tion for his speech in the Assembly, taking care not to appear to have learned anything from anybody. Obviously he will begin his speech with this introduction: 'From no one at any time, men of Athens, have I learned anything. Upon hearing that some men are competent in speaking and in public affairs, I have not tried to meet them. I have not taken the trouble to have an expert teach me—on the contrary! I have continued to avoid not only actually learning something from someone, but even the appearance of learning. Nevertheless, I shall give you whatever advice comes into my head automatic-ally.' It would be quite fitting also for men who want the office of public physician to introduce their speeches like that. They would have to begin their speeches as follows: 'From no one at any time, men of Athens, have I ever learned medicine. And I have not asked any doctor to become my teacher. I have continued to take the trouble not only to learn nothing from doctors but also to avoid the appearance of having learned this science. Nevertheless, give me the office of public physician. I shall try to experiment and learn with you.' " All those present laughed at the introduction. When it was clear **6** that Euthydemus was now paying attention to what Socrates was saying, but was still taking care not to say anything because he thought that his silence gave the appearance of wise self-control, Socrates then wanted to stop him from this and said, "Most amazing! The men who want to play a lyre or flute, to ride, or to become proficient in some similar skill, constantly practice what they want to master—and not just by themselves, but under the eyes of experts. They do everything and put up with everything, so as to do nothing without the guidance of these experts, for otherwise they cannot become worth noticing. Some of the men who wish to be able to speak and to engage in politics think that they will be able to do this suddenly and automatically, without preparation or study. And yet the small number of men who achieve success in **7** politics, as compared with the great number who engage in them, is commensurate with the difficulty of being successful in politics in comparison to the ease of the other skills. Clearly men who are interested in politics need more and better training than the men who are interested in the other arts." At **8** first, when Euthydemus listened, Socrates used to make remarks like the above, but when he perceived that Euthydemus was standing by more alertly, and was listening more eagerly when he talked, Socrates came to the saddler's shop by himself and when Euthydemus sat by him, he said, "Tell me, Euthydemus, have you really, as I hear, collected many of the writings of the men called wise?"

"Yes, by Zeus," replied Euthydemus, "And I still am collecting them, Socrates, until I have as many as I can."

"By Hera!" exclaimed Socrates. "I admire you because you **9** do not prefer treasures of gold and silver to wisdom! Clearly you believe that gold and silver do not make men better, but that the opinions of wise men enrich their owners with virtue." Euthydemus was very glad to hear this because he believed that Socrates thought he was on the right road to wisdom. Socrates saw that he was pleased with this praise, and said, "In what do you want to become proficient, when you make your choice of books?"

When Euthydemus was silent while he searched for a reply, Socrates again asked, "Do you wish then to become a physician? For there are many writings by physicians."

Euthydemus replied, "Not I, by Zeus!"

"Then do you want to become an architect? This also requires an experienced man."

"By no means," was the reply.

"Do you want to become a good mathematician like Theodorus?"

"No, not a mathematician."

"An astronomer?" continued Socrates, and the reply was "No."

"But not a rhapsodist? They say that you have the complete works of Homer."

"No, by Zeus," replied Euthydemus. "I know that rhapsodists know the epics perfectly, but they themselves are absolute fools."

"Can it be, Euthydemus, that you aspire to that virtue through which men become statesmen and householders, capable of ruling and helping other men as well as themselves?"

Euthydemus replied, "Socrates, this is the virtue I want the most."

"By Zeus, you want the highest virtue and the greatest art! For this is the art of kings, and is called 'The Royal Art.' Have you considered yet if it is possible to be good in ruling without being just?"

"Certainly. It is not even possible to be a good citizen without justice!"

"Then, no doubt, you have accomplished this?" asked Socrates.

"Socrates, I think that I do not appear to be less just than anyone."

"Are there duties appropriate to just men as there are duties appropriate to builders?" asked Socrates.

"Yes, there are."

"As builders have their works and products to exhibit, do the just have theirs to explain?"

Euthydemus said, "You are afraid that I cannot explain the works of justice! By Zeus, I can even explain the works of injustice, since there are not a few to be seen and heard every day!"

"Shall we then," continued Socrates, "write the letter 'J' here and the letter 'I' here? Then what we think are the works of justice, let us place under the 'J,' and under 'I,' let us place the works of injustice."   *13*

"If you think that is necessary, then do it," said Euthydemus. Socrates wrote the "I" and the "J" and said, "Does lying exist among men?"   *14*

"Certainly."

"Under which letter do we put lying?"

"Clearly," said Euthydemus, "under the 'I.'"

"Does deceit also exist?"

"Yes, indeed."

"Under which letter do we list deceit?"

"Clearly this also goes under 'I.'"

"What about evildoing?"

"This too," said Euthydemus.

"What about selling free men into slavery?" asked Socrates.

"That too."

"Won't any of these things be listed under 'J,' Euthydemus?" asked Socrates.

"That would be dreadful!"

"Why? Suppose a general captures and enslaves an unjust enemy state. Will we say that this is unjust?"   *15*

"Surely not," said Euthydemus.

"Won't we say that he does just deeds?"

"Surely," was Euthydemus' reply.

"What if he deceives them while fighting?"

"This," said Euthydemus, "is just."

"What if someone steals and plunders their goods? Isn't this just?" asked Socrates.

"Certainly!" said Euthydemus. "But I had assumed that you were asking this only in the case of friends."

"Therefore," said Socrates, "we must list under 'J' all the things we listed under 'I.'"

"So it seems," said Euthydemus.

16   "Then, please, now that we have listed them so, let us make a new distinction: it is just to do such things to enemies, and unjust to do them to friends. But with friends, a general must be as honest as possible."

"Yes," replied Euthydemus.

17   Socrates continued, "What if a general sees his troops demoralized and lies about reinforcements coming and, by this lie, puts an end to the soldiers' low morale? Under which letter shall we place this kind of deceit?"

"Under 'J,' I think."

"Suppose a man whose son needs medicine, and yet dislikes it, puts the medicine in his food somehow and so cures his son by making use of deceit. Where must this kind of deceit be listed?"

"I think," said Euthydemus, "this also goes in the same place."

"Suppose someone, when his friend is depressed, out of fear that his friend will commit suicide, steals or seizes his sword or some other such weapon. Where does this go?"

"This too, by Zeus, goes under 'J.'"

18   "Do you mean that you must not always deal openly in everything, even with your friends?"

"Surely not, by Zeus!" exclaimed Euthydemus. "I take back what I said before, if I may."

"Of course you must! Anything rather than to list it in the wrong place! But there is another factor we must not leave unexamined: In the case of men deceiving friends to their

19

detriment, which is more unjust, to do it willingly or to do it unwillingly?"

"Socrates, I really don't trust my own answers any longer. Everything that I said before now seems to be different from what I once thought. Nevertheless, let me answer that I think it is much more unjust to deceive a man willingly than unwillingly."

"Do you think that the teaching and knowledge of what is just is similar to the teaching and knowledge of grammar?"   20

"Yes, I do," replied Euthydemus.

"Who in your judgment is more literate? The man who intentionally writes and reads incorrectly or the man who is unintentionally incorrect?"

"The man who does so on purpose, I suppose, for he could, when he chooses, do this correctly."

"Therefore," continued Socrates, "the man who intentionally writes incorrectly is literate and the man who unintentionally writes incorrectly is illiterate?"

"How could it be otherwise?"

"Who knows what is just, the intentional liar and deceiver or the unintentional one?"

"Clearly, the intentional liar."

"You claim that the man who knows letters is more literate than the man who does not?"

"Yes."

"Then," continued Socrates, "is the man who knows what is just more just than the man who does not?"

"I seem to be saying so. But I think that I do not know what I mean!" replied Euthydemus.

"What about the man who wishes to speak the truth, but never says the same about the same things? When he tells you the road, for instance, he claims first that the road runs east, then that the same road goes west; or when he adds up an account, now the same figures total more, now less. What do you think of a man like that?"   21

"By Zeus, he obviously doesn't know what he thought he knew!"

22   "Do you know that some men are called slavish?"

"Yes, I do," replied Euthydemus.

"Why? Because of their wisdom or their ignorance [amathia]?" asked Socrates.

"Because of their ignorance, of course."

"Do they get this name because of their ignorance of metalwork?"

"Of course not!" exclaimed Euthydemus.

"Because of their ignorance of carpentry, perhaps?"

"No, not that!"

"Because of their ignorance of shoemaking?"

"Not because of that either. Rather, quite the opposite, for most of the men who are skilled in these trades are slavish."

"Then is ignorance the word used when men do not know the beautiful and the good and the just?" asked Socrates.

23   "I think so," said Euthydemus.

"Therefore, we must strive in every way to avoid being slaves."

Euthydemus said, "But by the gods, Socrates, I felt sure I was a philosopher studying the philosophy which would, I believed, give the right education for the man who desired to be truly noble! Now, how discouraged do you think I am when I see myself, after all my previous efforts, unable to answer questions which I ought to know, and with no road that I can follow in order to improve?"

24   Socrates replied, "Tell me, Euthydemus, have you ever gone to Delphi?"

"Twice, by Zeus."

"Did you notice the inscription on the temple somewhere that reads 'Know thyself'?"

"Yes."

"Did you pay no attention at all to the inscription? Or did you take heed and try to examine yourself and who you are?"

"By Zeus, surely not. I was certain that I knew this, for I would hardly know anything else if I did not know myself."

25   "Do you think a man knows himself who knows only his name? Or is the case like that of the men who buy horses, who

do not think that they know the horse they want to know until they have examined whether it is tame or wild, strong or weak, swift or slow, and how it is in all the other respects which make a horse useful or useless? Does not a man make this kind of examination as to what is his human use, and in this way come to know his own powers?"

"I think so," said Euthydemus, "The man who does not know his own powers does not know himself."

Socrates continued, "Is it not clear that through self-knowledge men experience most goods, and that they experience most evils because of self-deception? For men who know themselves know what they need, and they recognize what they can and cannot do. By doing what they know, they provide themselves with the things they need and they do them well. They avoid what they do not know; thus they do not make errors, and they avoid doing badly. On account of this, they are able to gauge other men, and through their dealings with others, they provide themselves with what is good and they guard against evils. Men who do not know, but are deceived in their own powers, are in the same predicament whether they face human beings or human enterprises. They do not know what they need or what they are doing or what they are dealing with. They make every sort of mistake, losing what is good and falling into evil. On the other hand, men who know what they are doing become famed and honored, for they are successful in what they do. Those who are like them gladly deal with them. Moreover, those who fail in their efforts ask them for advice and help; they put in such men all their hopes for good and, therefore, they feel a very special love for them. On the other hand, men who do not know what they are doing make bad choices and fail in whatever they try. Not only do they suffer losses and punishment in their efforts, but also they earn bad reputations, are ridiculed, and live despised and dishonored. You see this also in the case of states: all the states that do not know their own power and make war upon stronger states are either exterminated or become slaves without any freedom."

26
27
28
29

30   Euthydemus said, "Socrates, you may be sure that I am aware of how important self-knowledge is. But where should one begin the search? I look to you for the answer, if you are willing to tell me."

31   Socrates replied, "Do you have a thorough knowledge of what sort of things are good and what are bad?"

"By Zeus, if I did not know this, I would be baser than a slave!"

"Come," said Socrates, "tell me them."

"But it is not difficult. First, health itself is good, I believe, and sickness is bad. Then, of the causes of these conditions— drink, food, and habits—those that contribute to health are good while those that contribute to sickness are bad."

32   "Then," said Socrates, "health and sickness are good and bad according to when they are causes of good or evil?"

"When may health be the cause of evil and sickness the cause of good?" asked Euthydemus.

"When, by Zeus, there is a disastrous campaign or a fatal voyage and many similar incidents. The strong who take part in them perish, while those left behind because of ill health are safe."

"True. But you see," said Euthydemus, "that the strong also take part in successful enterprises and the weak are left behind."

"Then, since good and ill health are sometimes beneficial and sometimes harmful, are they any more good than bad?" asked Socrates.

33   "By Zeus, no! At least it seems so from this argument! But Socrates, there is no doubt that wisdom is good. For what is there that a wise man does not do better than a fool?"

"How so!" exclaimed Socrates. "Haven't you heard of Daedalus—how he was seized by Minos because of his wisdom and forced to serve him? He was deprived of his native land and his freedom. When he tried to escape with his son, he destroyed his son and could not himself be saved, but was carried off to the barbarians and again became a slave there."

"By Zeus," replied Euthydemus, "So the story is told!"

"Haven't you heard of the sufferings of Palamedes? Everyone sings hymns to him because he perished at the hands of Odysseus, who was envious of his wisdom."

"This, too, is the story told."

"How many others do you suppose have been stolen away by the Great King because of their wisdom, and there have become slaves?"

"Socrates, happiness most likely is an unquestionable good." 34

"O Euthydemus, if only it did not consist of so many questionable goods!"

"What in happiness could be called questionable?" asked Euthydemus.

"Nothing," said Socrates, "if you don't include beauty, strength, fame, or anything else of this sort in happiness!"

"But, by Zeus, we will include them. How would anyone become happy without these?"

"By Zeus, we shall then be including the cause of many of 35 men's difficulties. Many, because of their beauty, are ruined by admirers who have been driven to distraction by their good looks. Many, because of their strength, try deeds beyond their power and fall upon no small evil. Many, because of their wealth, are corrupted or victimized and so perish. Many, because of fame and political power, have suffered great evil."

"But if," said Euthydemus, "I am not correct in praising 36 happiness, I confess I do not know how I should pray to the gods!"

"Perhaps," said Socrates, "you did not examine these things because you were very confident that you knew them. Since you are preparing to direct a state that is a democracy, clearly you know what democracy is?"

"Certainly," he said.

"Do you think you can know what a democracy is without 37 knowing what the *demos* [people] is?"

"Of course not, by Zeus," replied Euthydemus.

"Do you know what the people is?"

"I do."

"And what do you consider the people to be?"

"I would say the poor citizens."

"Do you know who the poor are?"

"Of course!" replied Euthydemus.

"Then you know who the rich are?" asked Socrates.

"As well as I know who the poor are."

Socrates continued, "What sort of people do you call rich or poor?"

"By poor, I mean those who have not enough to pay for what they need; and by rich, those who have more than enough."

38   "Have you ever noticed," asked Socrates, "that some who have very little not only have enough, but even have a surplus, while some who have a great deal do not have enough?"

Euthydemus said, "By Zeus, you are right to remind me of this! I know that there are some tyrants who have been forced by their needs to commit crimes like the most desperate pauper."

39   "Then, as the argument stands," said Socrates, "we must classify some tyrants among the people, and some men who possess very little, as long as they economize, among the rich."

Euthydemus said, "Obviously my own lack of wit forces me to admit this, and I think it would be best for me to be silent! For I probably simply know nothing at all!" So Euthydemus went away discouraged, despising himself and considering himself really no better than a slave.

40   Many of the men who were treated like this by Socrates did not come near him again, and he considered them even more stupid. Euthydemus, however, realized that he would not become a worthwhile man unless he associated as much as he could with Socrates, and from that time on, he never left him unless some necessity arose. He even imitated some of Socrates' habits and pursuits. When Socrates understood that the young man was like this, he upset him as little as possible, and explained simply and clearly the knowledge he thought Euthydemus should have and the practices he considered most important.

Chapter 3: Socrates Converses with Euthydemus on Religion

Socrates was in no hurry to make his companions eloquent *1*
speakers, or men of action, or inventive geniuses. He thought
that they should first possess temperance. Men who had these
abilities without temperance only became more unjust and
more able to work evil, he believed. First of all he tried to *2*
make his companions moderate in regard to the gods. Other
men who were witnesses as he talked on this topic with various people have told their stories. I myself was present when
he spoke as follows with Euthydemus:

"Tell me, Euthydemus, have you ever come to observe how *3*
carefully the gods have prepared the needs of man?"

"By Zeus, I have not!"

"But don't you know that first and foremost we need light,
which the gods give us?"

"Yes, by Zeus, if we did not have light we would be like
blind men, as far as our eyes are concerned."

"And because we need rest they give us lovely night for our
rest."

"This too is a gift worth our gratitude," said Euthydemus.

"Because the sun shines and sheds light upon our daytime *4*
hours and all of our activities, whereas the night obscures
everything in darkness, they made stars shine in the night;
these mark the hours of the night, and enable us to do many
of the things we must do."

"This is so," he said.

"The moon marks for us the time not only of the night, but
also of the month."

"Yes," said Euthydemus.

"What of this? When we need food, the gods give food to us *5*
from the earth, and have arranged the seasons to furnish
abundantly not only all sorts of necessities but even delights."

"This, too," replied Euthydemus, "shows their love of mankind."

6 Socrates continued, "What of the fact that they give us water—which is so valuable that, with the aid of the earth and the seasons, it produces all that is useful to us? Water even nourishes us and, when mixed with all the things that give us nourishment, it makes them more digestible, more beneficial, and more palatable. Because we need water above everything else, they furnish it most abundantly."

"This too," said Euthydemus, "reveals their forethought."

7 "Haven't they given us fire, a defense against cold and darkness, a fellow worker, as it were, in every art and in the preparation of every artifact that man uses? In short, man makes nothing worthwhile and useful in life without fire."

"This is the supreme instance of their love of mankind!" replied Euthydemus.

8 "Consider how, when the sun crosses the winter solstice and approaches, some fruits ripen and others wither because their season is over. When the sun's work is accomplished, doesn't it stop drawing nearer and turn away, to avoid harming us by heating us more than we need? When the sun withdraws to the point where, clearly, we would be frozen with cold if it went farther off, doesn't it turn again, advance, and traverse the part of the heavens where it may benefit us most?"

"By Zeus," exclaimed Euthydemus, "all of this, as well, seems to have been brought about for man's sake!"

9 Socrates continued, "Since we clearly could not endure heat or cold if it occurred suddenly, do you see how the sun approaches and withdraws little by little, so that we fail to notice how we arrived at either extreme?"

"Now I wonder," said Euthydemus, "if there is any other function for the gods except to serve man. But what prevents me from thinking this is the fact that all animals share these benefits."

10 "Isn't it also clear," said Socrates, "that animals are born and raised for the sake of man? What other living being except man enjoys so many goods from goats, sheep, cattle,

horses, and asses, among other animals? For I think that man derives more goods from animals than from plants; or, at any rate, men are nourished and enriched no less from animals than from plants. Many men do not use the fruits of the earth for food, but live upon the milk, cheese, and meat from their livestock. All men tame and domesticate useful animals and use them for war and many other purposes."

"I agree with you, Socrates, because I see animals much stronger than man so dominated by man as to be used as men wish."

"Consider the many different kinds of beautiful and useful   11
things. Hasn't man been endowed with perceptions suited to this variety through which we can enjoy every kind of good? The gods have endowed us with reason, by which we think about what we perceive, remember it, and come to understand how it is useful. Then we contrive many ways of enjoying good and of avoiding evil. They give us the power of speech,   12
by which we share all the good things with one another through teaching, and by which we form communities, pass laws, and become citizens of a state."

"Socrates, the gods truly seem to show great concern for men in all these respects."

Socrates continued, "What of the fact that, whereas we are powerless to foresee what will be of advantage in the future, the gods themselves, when we inquire, aid us by revealing through divination what will come about, and by teaching us how events may turn out in the best way possible?"

"They seem to treat you, Socrates, with more love than they treat other men, if it is true that they tell you what to do and what not to do without your asking."

"You yourself will realize that I speak the truth, if you do   13
not wait until you see their outward and visible forms, but, because you see their works, are satisfied to revere and to honor the gods. Note that the gods themselves teach this by their example, for when they give us gifts, the other gods do not present them in person, nor does the one god, who controls and orders the whole universe in which everything is good and beautiful, and who offers, for our use, goods that are

fresh, whole, and new—goods which, quicker than thought, serve us unerringly. This god is manifest in performing these great works, and yet while he administers them he is invisible to us. Note also that even the sun, which seems to appear to all, does not allow men to look at it carefully. If someone tries to stare boldly at the sun he will lose his sight. You will find that the god's agents are also invisible: The thunderbolt, for example, clearly comes from on high and overpowers all whom it strikes. Yet we cannot see it come or strike or go away. Not even the winds are visible, yet their effects are obvious and we perceive them as they come. Indeed, even the soul of man—which, more than all else that is human, shares in the divine—cannot be seen; yet clearly the soul rules us. We must understand this and not despise what we cannot see; and, realizing their power from its effects, we must honor the divine.

15 "Socrates," said Euthydemus, "I know clearly that I shall by no means neglect the divine, but I feel discouraged when I realize that no one can ever return thanks worthy of the gods' benefits."

16 "Don't be discouraged, Euthydemus. For you see that when someone asked the god at Delphi how he might return thanks to the gods, the god replied, 'According to the law of the state.' Surely the law everywhere is that a man should propitiate the gods with sacrifices according to his power. How then would anyone honor the gods more excellently or more reverently *17* than by doing as the gods themselves command? But he must not do less than is in his power; otherwise, when someone does less than he can, he is clearly not honoring the gods. Therefore, when a man does all in his power to honor the gods, he should take heart and hope for the greatest goods. A man could be called temperate when he does not hope for greater goods from anyone except from those who are able to bestow the greatest benefits, and there is no other way to achieve this except by pleasing them. How could he better please the *18* gods than by obeying them as best he can?" By such words and deeds, Socrates made his companions more reverent and more temperate.

Chapter 4: Hippias of Elis and Socrates' Method of Definition

On the subject of justice, also, Socrates did not conceal his opinions, but he made them evident even by his deeds. In his private life, he dealt with everyone lawfully and helpfully; and in his public life, he was obedient to the leaders in all that the laws required, in both civil and military life. He was, thus, a clear example of good discipline when compared to other men. When he became president [*epistates*] of the Assemblies,[1] for example, he did not allow the people to vote contrary to the law, but, with the laws as his aid, he opposed the people's rage—which was so great that, I think, no other man would have withstood it. Also, when the Thirty Tyrants[2] ordered him to do something contrary to the law, he did not obey. They forbade him to talk with the young men and they commanded him, along with some other citizens, to arrest a man to be put to death; but Socrates alone did not obey because the order was illegal.[3] Other men in trials customarily appeal to the jurors for favors, flatter them, and plead illegally, and through such behavior many frequently are freed by the jurors; yet when he was indicted by Meletus, Socrates was not willing to play any of the usual illegal tricks in court. He would have been acquitted easily by the jurors had he followed these practices just a little. However, he preferred to die abiding by the law than to live by breaking the law. He often spoke on the subject of justice with various people, and I myself know how he once held the following discussion of

1

2

3

4

5

1 See note 7, p. 7.
2 See note 7, p. 13.
3 Plato tells this story in detail: *Apology* 32c–d.

justice with Hippias of Elis.[4] Hippias, who had come to Athens after being away for a time, came upon Socrates just as he was saying to some men how amazing it was that, if a man wanted to learn shoemaking or building or metalwork or riding, he had no trouble finding where to go to learn the craft. "Some," he continued, "even say that if you want to train a horse or an ox to do the right thing, the place is full of teachers. Yet if someone wants to learn justice or to have his son or slave taught justice, he does not know where to go

6   and get this knowledge." Hippias heard and exclaimed jokingly, "Socrates, are you still saying the very same things I once heard long ago from you?"

"What is still more dreadful, Hippias, I am always saying not only the same things, but also on the same subjects! I suppose that you are so very learned that you never say the same thing on the same subject!"

"By all means, yes!" replied Hippias. "I am always trying to say something new."

7   "Do you mean about what you know? If, for example, someone asks you how many letters are in Socrates' name and what they are, do you try to give different answers at different times? Or take the example of numbers: if a man asks if two times five are ten, don't you give the same answer that you gave before?"

"Socrates," said Hippias, "just like you, I give the same answer about such subjects. Yet on the subjects of justice, I think I have something to say now to which neither you nor anyone else can object."

8   "By Hera!" said Socrates, "You mean you have found such a great good! Juries will cease to split their vote; citizens will stop wrangling, going to court, and raising revolts in the cause of justice. States will cease to differ about what is just, and

---

4 Hippias was an early enemy of specialization who was able to lecture on anything. He made his point about universal knowledge by appearing at Olympia elegantly dressed with everything from shoes to finger ring of his own making.

cease to make war. I do not know how I could leave you before hearing of your great discovery."

Hippias said, "By Zeus, you shall not hear it until you yourself have stated what you believe justice is! For we have had enough of you laughing at others and questioning them and making objections, while you yourself are not willing to give an account to anyone or state your opinion on any subject." 9

"Why, Hippias! Haven't you observed that I never cease to demonstrate what I think justice is?" 10

"And what kind of an account of justice is that?"

"If I don't give an account by words, certainly I teach it by deeds. Don't you think that deeds are better evidence than words?"

"Much better, by Zeus!" replied Hippias. "Many who say just words commit injustices, while no one who does just deeds would ever be unjust." 11

"Have you ever observed me bearing false witness, or blackmailing, or inciting friends or fellow citizens to rebellion, or doing any other injustice?"

"I have not," replied Hippias.

"Do you not think it is just to refrain from injustices?"

"Socrates, now you are clearly trying to avoid stating an opinion as to what you think justice is! For you are saying what just men do not do, not what they do!"

"But," said Socrates, "I think that to be unwilling to commit injustice is a sufficient definition of justice. However, if you don't think so, see if this is enough for you: I state that justice is what is lawful." 12

"Do you mean that *lawful* and *just* are the same?"

"I do," replied Socrates.

"I do not understand what you mean by the terms *lawful* and *just*." 13

"Do you know the laws of a state?"

"Yes," said Hippias.

"What do you think they are?" said Socrates.

"What the citizens in a body enact as to what should be done, and what should not."

"Then," said Socrates, "a man is law-abiding if he lives in the state according to these laws, and lawless if he breaks them?"

"Certainly."

"Then the man who obeys the laws does what is just, and the man who disobeys does what is unjust."

"Yes," replied Hippias.

"Therefore, the man who does just deeds is just, and the man who does unjust deeds is unjust?"

"How could it be otherwise?"

"Therefore, the law-abiding man is just, and the lawless man is unjust."

14   Hippias replied, "Socrates, how can laws or obedience to the laws be considered a serious matter when the people who make them often reject them and change them?"

"Well," replied Socrates, "likewise states often declare war and then make peace again."

"Yes," said Hippias.

"Do you think there is any difference between deprecating men who obey the laws because the laws may be abolished, and scorning those who are well disciplined in war because peace may come? Or do you blame the men who are eager to help their countries in time of war?"

"By Zeus, no!" said Hippias.

15   "Have you really understood about Lycurgus the Lacedaemonian—that he would not have made Sparta any different from other states had he not, first and foremost, set obedience to the law on a firm basis there? Don't you realize that in states the rulers who are most responsible for making the citizens obey the law are the best, and that the state in which the citizens are the most law-abiding flourishes the most in

16   peace, and is invincible in war? Unity seems to be the most important good for states; most often, in states, the senates and noblest men urge their people to unity. Everywhere in Greece, the law enjoins the people to swear to unity, and everywhere they swear this oath. This occurs, I think, not so that the citizens may vote for the same choruses, praise the

same flute-players, choose the same poets, or enjoy the same pleasures, but so that they may obey the law. For when the citizens abide by the law, the states are strongest and most prosperous. Without unity, a state is not well governed or a house well run. In private life, how could anyone suffer less from his state, or win more honor, than by obeying the law? How could he suffer less in court; what better way is there to win a case? To whom would anyone prefer to entrust his wealth or his sons or daughters? Who would the whole state think is more trustworthy than the law-abiding man? From whom would anyone—whether parent, relative, slave, friend, citizen, or foreigner—more expect to receive justice? Whom would the enemy trust more in arranging a truce or treaty, or the terms of peace? Whom would they prefer to have as an ally? To whom would allies prefer to entrust leadership, a command, or even their states? Whom would a benefactor expect to return a favor more than the law-abiding man, and whom would anyone prefer to help than the man from whom he thinks he will receive recompense? To whom would anyone prefer to be a friend than to such a man? To whom would anyone less want to be an enemy? With whom would anyone be less likely to wage war than with the man whom he really wants to be his friend, not his enemy, and with whom most people want alliances and friendships, and only a very few war and enmity? Hippias, now I have demonstrated that the lawful and the just are the same. If you have objections to raise, tell us!"

Hippias said, "But by Zeus, Socrates, I do not think I have an objection to raise to what you have said about justice!"

"Do you know any unwritten laws, Hippias?"

"Those at any rate that are observed in every country in the same way?" said Hippias.

"Could you say that men made them?"

Hippias replied, "How could men have made them, when all men cannot meet together and all men do not speak the same language?"

"Who do you believe made these laws?"

"On the basis of the fact that among all men it is the law to worship the gods, I believe that the gods made these laws for men."

20 "Is it the law everywhere to honor parents?"

"Yes," replied Hippias.

"And to forbid marriage between parents and children?"

"No, Socrates, I no longer think that this is a law of god."

"But why?" asked Socrates.

"Because I perceive that there are some who break this law."

21 "But there are many other laws that are broken. Yet men who break laws ordained by the gods pay a penalty which they cannot escape in any way at all as some do when they break man-made laws and yet escape punishment through stealth or violence."

22 "What, Socrates, is the inescapable penalty of incestuous sexual intercourse?"

"By Zeus, the heaviest of penalties! What greater penalty could a man pay than to beget ill-begotten offspring!"

23 "How are offspring ill-begotten when nothing prevents those who are of good stock from producing good stock?"

"Because, by Zeus," replied Socrates, "not only must people be of good stock to produce good stock, but they must also be in their physical prime. Do you imagine that the seed of parents in their prime is like the seed of those not yet in their prime, or else past it?"

"By Zeus, it is likely that they are not the same!"

"Which is better?"

"Plainly, the seed of those in their prime."

"Then the seed of men not in their prime is not good?"

"Most likely not, by Zeus," replied Hippias.

"Then children should not be produced that way?"

"No," said Hippias.

"Therefore, those who beget children in this way ought not to do so?" asked Socrates.

"I agree," said Hippias.

"Who else except them would produce ill-begotten children?"

"I agree with you there as well."

"What then of this: isn't it the custom everywhere to return good for good?"

24

"It is the custom, but a custom which also is broken."

"Don't those who break this custom pay a penalty by losing their good friends and being forced to run after the men who hate them? Isn't this the way it happens: those who treat their acquaintances well are good friends, while those who do not return favors become hated because of their ingratitude, and yet run after the men who treated them well even more eagerly because they profit so much by them?"

"By Zeus, Socrates, all these cases seem to concern the laws of gods. Laws which involve their own punishments to those who break them are better laws than those made by human legislators, I think."

"Hippias, do you think that the gods legislate just laws or laws that are other than just?"

25

"Not laws that are other than just, by Zeus! For if the gods did not legislate just laws, who else would?"

"Hippias, the gods therefore are satisfied that *just* and *lawful* are the same thing."

Thus, by words and actions, Socrates made those near him more just.

Chapter 5: Socrates and Euthydemus Discuss Self-control

Socrates also made his companions more active and enterprising, as I shall now explain. Because he himself believed that self-control was good to have if a man intended to achieve some good goal, first of all, he was a clear example to his companions of a man who had disciplined himself more than anyone, and secondly, in his discussions, he urged his companions to turn toward self-control before all else. He continually kept before his own mind, and that of his companions, what was useful in gaining excellence. I know that once he had the following discussion with Euthydemus about self-control.

"Tell me, Euthydemus, do you think that freedom is a noble and important possession for man and state?"

"How could any possession be nobler or more important?"

3   "When a man is ruled by bodily pleasures and on account of them cannot do the best deeds, do you think he is free?"

"He is the least free possible!" replied Euthydemus.

"Perhaps you would agree that freedom is doing the best deeds, and next, you believe that to have masters who prevent one from doing the best deeds is to be without freedom?"

"By all means!"

4   "Are you in complete agreement with the opinion that the intemperate are not free?"

"By Zeus, of course!"

"Do you think that the intemperate are prevented from doing the best deeds, or that they are forced to do the worst deeds?"

"They are no less forced to do the worst deeds than they are prevented from doing the best deeds!" said Euthydemus.

5   "What kind of masters are they, do you think, who prevent the best and require the worst?"

"By Zeus, the worst possible!" exclaimed Euthydemus.

"What kind of slavery do you consider the worst?" asked Socrates.

"That under the worst masters, I would say," replied Euthydemus.

"Then intemperate men serve the worst slavery?"

"I think so," said Euthydemus.

6   "Don't you think that intemperance, by keeping men from the greatest good, wisdom, drives them to the opposite? Don't you agree that intemperance prevents men from paying attention to what is useful and from coming to an understanding of this by attracting them to pleasures; and even when men are well aware of good and evil, intemperance, by confusing these, makes men choose something worse in place of something better?"

"Yes," he said, "This happens."

"Euthydemus, would you say there is anyone who has less
temperance than the intemperate man? That the effects of
temperance and of intemperance are complete opposites?"
continued Socrates.

"I agree with this also."

"Is there anything more effective than intemperance in preventing a man from attending to what he ought to do?"

"There is not," replied Euthydemus.

"Do you think that there is anything worse for man than
that which causes him to choose harm instead of good, pre-
vails on him to neglect good and care for evil, and forces him
to do the opposite of what temperate people do?"

"There is nothing worse."

"Isn't it likely that self-control has effects on men that are
opposite to the effects of lack of self-control?"

"Certainly," replied Euthydemus.

"And that the effects that are opposite to the effects of lack
of self-control are presumably the best?"

"Yes, it is likely."

"Then, Euthydemus, isn't self-control best for men?"

"Yes, Socrates, it is likely."

"I wonder, Euthydemus, whether you have ever thought to
notice something."

"What?"

"That intemperance cannot lead men to the very pleasures
to which it is supposed to lead them, while self-control makes
men enjoy all pleasures to the fullest."

"How is that?" asked Euthydemus.

"Intemperance does not allow us to resist hunger or thirst
or sexual desire or sleepiness; and since it is only by waiting
or restraining themselves until the moment when the greatest enjoyment is possible that men can derive full pleasure
from eating, drinking, sexual intercourse, rest, and sleep, intemperance prevents men from enjoying to any extent worth
mentioning the most natural and elementary pleasures. On
the other hand, self-control alone makes men resist the above-

mentioned desires, and thus produces pleasures worth remembering."

"What you say is quite true."

10   "Learning something beautiful and good and taking the trouble to train the body well, to manage a household capably, to be
useful to friends and to the state, to overcome enemies—these
are indeed the source of the highest pleasures, as well as of
useful pleasures. Self-controlled men find enjoyment in doing
these good deeds, but intemperate men have no share in them.
Could we say that anyone has less to do with the pleasures
just mentioned than the man who cannot perform good deeds
because he is confined to pursuing the pleasures nearest at
hand?"

11   Euthydemus said, "I think, Socrates, that you mean that the
man who is completely in the power of bodily pleasures has
nothing to do with virtue."

"What difference is there between the intemperate man and
the crudest beast? What difference is there between the most
senseless animal and the man who does not aim for the highest goals, but tries in every way he can to follow his pleasure?
Only the self-controlled can aim for the highest goals, and
can, in word and deed, choose good and avoid evil, after hav-
12   ing divided them according to their class. So it is that they become the noblest and happiest men and the most capable in
dialectic. For," he continued, "the word 'dialectic' comes from
peoples' coming together to deliberate by dividing [*dialegein*]
things according to their class. Therefore, a man must try as
best he can to prepare himself in dialectic and to pursue it as
much as possible. For this is the way that men become the
noblest, the best in leading men, and the most skilled in
dialectic."

Chapter 6: Illustrations of Socrates' Method of Definition

1   I shall now try to tell how Socrates made his companions
excel in dialectic. He believed that men who knew what each

individual being was could explain it to the others. As for those who do not know this, it did not surprise him that they made mistakes and caused others to make mistakes. This is why he never ceased investigating with his companions what each individual being was. Because it would be a great task to explain thoroughly how he defined everything, I shall tell only as much as will make clear his method of investigation. First, he used to analyze reverence something like this:

2

"Tell me, Euthydemus, what sort of thing do you think reverence is?"

"By Zeus, a most excellent thing."

"Can you tell me what kind of man the reverent man is?"

"I think he honors the gods."

"Is it possible to honor the gods in any way one wishes?"

"No. There are laws according to which one must honor the gods."

"Does the man who knows these laws know how to honor the gods?"

3

"I think so," said Euthydemus.

"And does the man who knows how he must honor the gods also think that he must do as he knows he ought, and not otherwise?" asked Socrates.

"Yes."

"Does anyone honor the gods other than as he thinks he ought?"

"I think not."

"Will the man, then, who knows what is lawful in regard to the gods honor the gods lawfully?"

4

"Certainly."

"Does the man who honors the gods lawfully honor them as he ought?"

"Of course."

"And the man who honors them as he ought is reverent?"

"Certainly."

"Then we may conclude that a reverent man may rightly be defined as the man who knows the law in regard to the gods."

"To me, at least, it seems so," said Euthydemus.

5   "May a man deal with men in any way he wishes?"

"No. In regard to men, too, there are laws according to which men must deal with one another."

"Do men who deal with one another according to these laws act as they ought?"

"How could it be otherwise!"

"Do men who deal with others as they ought treat them well?"

"Certainly," replied Euthydemus.

"Do those who treat men well behave well in human affairs?"

"It is likely."

"Do men who obey the law do just deeds?" asked Socrates.

"Certainly."

6   "Do you know what kind of things are called just?"

"What the laws command," he replied.

"Do men who do what the laws command do what is just and what they ought?"

"How could it be otherwise!"

"Are men who do just deeds, just men?"

"I think so."

"Do you think that anyone obeys the laws without knowing what the laws command?"

"No," replied Euthydemus.

"Do you think that anyone who knows what he ought to do thinks that he should not do it?"

"I do not."

"Do you know anyone who does other than what he thinks he ought to do?"

"I do not," replied Euthydemus.

"Do men who know the law in regard to mankind do just deeds?"

"Certainly."

"Are men who do just deeds, just men?" asked Socrates.

"Who else would be?"

"Then our definition is correct which defines just men as those who know the law in regard to mankind?"

"I think so."

"What shall we say wisdom is?" continued Socrates. "Tell   7
me, do you think the wise are wise in what they know, or in
what they do not know?"

"Obviously, in what they know," replied Euthydemus. "How
could a man be wise in things he does not know?"

"Then the wise are wise in knowledge?" asked Socrates.

"In what else would a man be wise, if not in knowledge?"

"Do you think that wisdom is something other than that by
which men are wise?"

"No!" replied Euthydemus.

"Then wisdom is knowledge?" asked Socrates.

"I think so."

"Do you think a man can know everything that exists?"

"By Zeus, no! Not even the slightest fraction!" said Euthydemus.

"Then a man cannot be wise in everything?" asked Socrates.

"By Zeus, surely not!"

"Whatever each man knows, is it in this that he is wise?"

"I think so."

"Euthydemus, shouldn't we now seek the good in this way?"   8
asked Socrates.

"In what way?"

"Do you think that the same thing is useful to all?"

"I do not."

"What, then? Don't you think that what is useful to one
man may sometimes be harmful to another?"

"Yes indeed!"

"Would you say," continued Socrates, "that the good is
something different from the useful?"

"No!"

"The useful, then, is good to whomever it may be useful?"

"So it seems."

"Could we say anything different in regard to the beautiful?   9
Can you name a body or a utensil, or anything else, which you
know is beautiful in every respect?"

"By Zeus, I cannot!"

"Then the beauty in each thing lies in its use for whatever purpose it is useful?"

"Certainly."

"And does a thing's beauty lie in anything else except in the purpose for which it is used?"

"No, nowhere else."

"The useful, then, is beautiful for any purpose for which it is useful?"

"I think so."

10   "Euthydemus, turning now to courage, do you consider courage one of the things that are beautiful?"

"The most beautiful!" was his reply.

"Do you consider courage useful for no small purpose?"

"By Zeus, it is useful for the greatest purpose!"

"Do you think that, in the midst of terrors and dangers, it is useful to be unaware of them?"

"Not in the least!"

"When men do not fear such dangers because they are not aware of what they are, are they courageous?"

"By Zeus, no!" said Euthydemus, "that way many madmen and cowards would be courageous."

"What of the men who fear what is not fearful?" asked Socrates.

"They are even less courageous, by Zeus."

"Then you believe that the men who are good in the face of terrors and dangers are courageous and the men who are bad in the face of these are cowards?"

"Certainly."

11   "Do you think that any are good in the face of terrors except the men who are able to deal with them well?"

"None but these," replied Euthydemus.

"And bad, except those who deal with them badly?" continued Socrates.

"Who else could be?"

"Does each man conduct himself as he thinks he ought?"

"How else?" answered Euthydemus.

"Do men who cannot conduct themselves well know how they ought to behave?"

"Certainly not."

"Then the men who know how they ought to behave are the men who can do so?"

"They are the only ones!"

"What of this? Do men who have not blundered completely conduct themselves badly in these situations?"

"I think not."

"And those who conduct themselves badly have made blunders?"

"It is likely."

"Finally, then, are those who know how to conduct themselves well in the face of dangers and terrors courageous; and are those who are completely mistaken cowards?"

"So they seem to me," replied Euthydemus.

Socrates was of the opinion that kingship and tyranny were both forms of government, but he believed they differed from each other. Kingship is the government of men both with their consent and according to laws of the state, he said, while tyranny is government both without the consent of the people and not according to law, but as the ruler wishes. Where magistrates are chosen from among the men who discharge their lawful obligations, the state, he believed, is an aristocracy. Where the magistrates are chosen on the basis of property, the government is a plutocracy, and where the officials are chosen from among all the citizens, it is a democracy. 12

Whenever a man argued with him on some subject and had nothing clear to say, but without proof simply alleged that this man or that man whom he named was wiser, a better politician, braver, or whatever else, Socrates would bring the whole discussion back to the basic assumption as follows: 13

"Do you say that the man you are praising is a better citizen than the man I am praising?" 14

"Yes, I do."

"Then why don't we first consider the question of what the function of a good citizen is?"

"Let us do that!"

"In the administration of finance, isn't the better man the one who makes the city wealthier?"

"Certainly!"

"In war, isn't the better man the one who makes the state stronger than the enemy?"

"How could it be otherwise!"

"In diplomacy, isn't he better who makes friends for his state instead of enemies?"

"Quite likely."

"And in debate," continued Socrates, "the man who stops rebellion and promotes unity?"

"I think so."

15   By developing the argument this way, the truth became evident to the men who were arguing against him. Whenever he conducted an argument, he proceeded step by step from one point of agreement to the next because he believed that this made the argument certain. Whenever he argued, therefore, he gained more agreement than did anyone I know. He said that Homer conferred on Odysseus the title of "safe orator" [1] because he was skilled in leading his arguments from one accepted opinion to the next.

Chapter 7: Socrates' Theories of Education

1   I think that I have shown in what has been said that Socrates stated his opinion frankly and simply to those who conversed with him. I shall now tell how Socrates took great pains to give men an independent spirit in the activities for which they were suited. Of all the men I know, I never knew one who took such care to know in what field one of his companions was really versed. As far as he had knowledge, he was most eager to teach all that was fitting for a truly noble man to know. Where he lacked the knowledge, he took his friends

2   to those who had it. He also taught how much a well-edu-

[1] *Odyssey* VIII. 171.

cated person should know about a given subject. In geometry, for example, he said that a man should learn enough to be able to measure land correctly, in case he ever had to take possession of, convey, divide, or calculate the yield of crops. This was so easy to learn that anyone who put his mind to surveying land could soon leave with a knowledge of how big the land was and how it is measured. He did not approve of *3* learning geometry to the point of studying complicated diagrams. He said he could not see what use these had—not that he himself did not know them; but he said that they could consume the lifetime of a man to the exclusion of many other useful studies. He was insistent that men should have a prac- *4* tical knowledge of astronomy—enough to tell the time of night, of the month, or of the year; thus, through distinguishing such times, a man might have good evidence of the time while he was traveling by land or sea, or arranging guard duty or performing all the other activities that take place by night, by the month, or by the year. This much is easy to learn from night hunters, pilots, and many others whose business it is to know this. He strongly disapproved of pursuing the study of *5* astronomy so far as to include knowing the bodies that revolve in different courses, the planets, and the comets, and spending one's life calculating their distances from the earth, their cycles, and the causes of these cycles. He said he saw no use in these studies, although he had heard lectures on these subjects; but he said these also could consume a lifetime to the exclusion of many useful studies. *6*

In general, he turned his back on becoming one who speculates on how the god contrives the heavenly phenomena. He believed that man could not discover this, and he thought that the gods were displeased with the man who asked about what they did not want to disclose. He said that the man who concerned himself with these studies ran the risk of going out of his mind, as did Anaxagoras, who was insanely proud of his explanation of the divine mechanism. Anaxagoras said that *7* fire and the sun were the same thing; he was unaware that man can easily look upon fire, but cannot gaze steadily on the sun, and that the skin is blackened by the light of the sun, but not by the light of fire. He was not aware that the plants of the earth cannot grow well without the rays of the sun, while everything is burned and ruined by fire. He alleged that the sun was a fiery stone and did not know that stone in a fire does not glow and does not resist the fire for long, while the sun forever remains the most brilliant of all objects.

8 Similarly, Socrates insisted that men should study arithmetic and, as in other studies, he insisted that men should avoid vain activity. As far as a study was useful, he joined in investigating it and pursued it with his companions.

9 He strongly urged his companions to watch out for their health by learning as much as they could from experts. He also advised them to watch throughout their lives what food, drink, and exercise helped them and how to use these in such a way as to be as healthy as possible. By taking care of themselves this way, he said, it would be a hard task to find a doctor who could diagnose better than themselves what helped their health.

10 Whenever anyone wanted help that human wisdom could not give, Socrates advised him to turn to divination, because, he said, the man who knows the means by which the gods make their revelations to men will never lack the counsel of the gods.

Chapter 8: Socrates' Death

1 If anyone thinks that Socrates is proven to have lied about his *daimon* because the jury condemned him to death when he declared that a divinity revealed to him what he should and should not do, let him note two facts: First, that he was so far advanced in age that he would have died soon, if not then; and second, that he escaped the bitterest part of life, when all men's mental powers diminish.[1] Instead of this, he won glory for the strength of soul that he displayed when he

---

[1] Cf. *Socrates' Defense Before the Jury* 6–7 (p. 146).

spoke as truthfully, freely, and justly as possible, bearing the
sentence of death with the greatest gentleness and manliness.
For it is an admitted fact that no one in the memory of man   2
ever bore death more nobly. He was forced to live thirty days
after sentence was pronounced; for it was the time of the
Delia,[2] and the law does not allow any public executions until
the embassy returns from Delos. During this time, as all of his
companions could see, he lived as he had lived previously.
Even before that time he had always amazed all men by the
cheerfulness and serenity with which he lived.

How could anyone die more nobly than this? What death   3
could be nobler than the death a man meets as nobly as possible? What death could be happier than the noblest death?
What death could be dearer to the gods than the happiest
death?

I shall tell you what I heard Hermogenes, the son of Hip-   4
ponicus, say about him.[3] Hermogenes said that after Meletus
had already filed his indictment, he himself heard Socrates discussing everything except his trial; Hermogenes told him that
he ought to be thinking about what defense he should make.
Socrates first replied, "Don't you think that I have spent my
life practicing this?" When Hermogenes asked him how, he
said that he had never done anything else but to examine what
things were just and unjust, and to do justice and avoid injustice—which he thought was the finest possible practice for
his defense. When Hermogenes returned to the subject and   5
said, "Don't you realize, Socrates, that Athenian juries have
put many innocent men to death because they were misled by
a speech, and that they have freed many criminals?"

Socrates said, "But by Zeus, Hermogenes, just now when I

---

[2] A festival held annually when the Athenians sent a ship to Delos to
honor Apollo in gratitude for the safe return of Theseus and the fourteen young men and women whom he saved from the Minotaur in Crete.
As long as the mission was away, the city had to be kept pure of public
executions. Plato informs us (*Phaedo* 58b) that the ship was sent the
day before the trial.

[3] Cf. the account in *Socrates' Defense* 2 ff.; see also Introduction, pp.
xii–xv.

tried to consider my defense before the jurors, my *daimon* opposed it."

6 "Extraordinary!" said Hermogenes. But Socrates said, "Are you amazed if the god thinks it better for me to end my life now? Don't you know that I would never admit that, up to now, any man has lived a better or more pleasant life than mine? I think that the men who are most concerned with becoming as good as possible live the noblest lives; and those who perceive most fully that they have become as good as possible live the most pleasant lives. I have perceived that up to now this has happened to me. When I meet other men and compare myself to them, I continue to have this opinion of myself. And not only I, but also my friends, continue to have this opinion of me; not because they love me (for then they would have this opinion about all the rest of their friends), but because they think that they too, by being with me, become as good as possible. If I am to live longer, perhaps I must live out my old age, seeing and hearing less, understanding worse, coming to learn with more difficulty and to be more forgetful, and growing worse than those to whom I was once superior. Indeed, life would be unliveable, even if I did not notice the change; and if I see the change, how could life not be even more wretched and unpleasant?

9 "If I am to die unjustly, this will be the disgrace of those who put me to death unjustly. If to do injustice is a disgrace, how could it not be a disgrace to do something unjust? What disgrace is it to me that other people could not decide or act justly in my case? I see that even the fame of our forefathers does not remain the same in posterity, but varies according to whether they suffered injustice, or else committed it. I do know that, if I die now, I shall obtain a different recognition from what the men who put me to death will receive. For I know that men will always testify that I never wronged any man and never made a man evil, but always tried to make my companions better." This is what he said to Hermogenes and the others.

11 Of all who know Socrates and what he was like, all those

who seek virtue even now continue to long for him, for he was the most helpful in aiding them in their quest for virtue. To me, as I describe what Socrates was like, he was so reverent that he could do nothing without counsel from the gods; so just that he never hurt anyone at all, but aided all who dealt with him; so self-controlled that he never chose pleasures in place of something better; so prudent that he never erred in distinguishing what was better from what was worse, and he never needed another's counsel, but was independent in his decisions about good and evil. He was skilled in arguing and in defining good and evil, and skilled in testing others, showing them their mistakes, and urging them toward virtue and true nobility. He seemed to be what the noblest and happiest man would be. And if anyone is not satisfied with this, let him compare the character of other men with what I have described, and then let him judge.

SOCRATES' DEFENSE
BEFORE THE JURY

SOCRATES' DEFENSE
BEFORE THE JURY

I think it worthwhile to remember Socrates and how he
planned for his defense and the end of his life when he was
summoned before the court. Others also have written about
this and all have noticed Socrates' grandiloquent manner of
speaking—which is clear proof that he really spoke that way.
But these writers have not made clear the fact that Socrates
had already come to consider death preferable to life, and
thus they have made his grandiloquence seem rather senseless.
Nevertheless Hermogenes, the son of Hipponicus,[1] was a companion of Socrates, and his reports about Socrates are such
that they make his grandiloquent speech appear fitting and
purposeful. Hermogenes said, when he saw Socrates discussing
everything except his trial, "Socrates, shouldn't you be thinking about how you will make your defense? "

Socrates first replied, "Don't you think that I have spent my
life practicing my defense? " When Hermogenes asked how,
he continued, "Because I have not done any injustice—which
I think is the finest possible practice for my defense."

When Hermogenes returned to the subject again, he said,
"Don't you realize that the Athenian juries have often put
innocent men to death because they were misled by a speech,
and that they have often freed criminals because a speech
aroused their pity or gave them pleasure?"

Socrates replied, "But, by Zeus, twice already when I tried
to think about my defense, my *daimon* opposed it."

"Extraordinary!" said Hermogenes, but Socrates replied,
"Do you think it extraordinary if even the god thinks it better

1 Cf. IV. 8. 4, and Introduction, pp. xii–xv.

for me to die now? Don't you know that I would never admit that, up to now, any man has spent a better life than I? I say this because it is the most gratifying thing to know that I have always lived a just and holy life. Therefore, I have great self-esteem, and I find that my friends also have formed the same opinion about me.

6   "If my life is to be prolonged now, I know that I must live out my old age, seeing worse, hearing less, learning with more difficulty, and forgetting more and more of what I have learned. If I see myself growing worse and reproach myself for
7   it, tell me, how could I continue to live pleasantly? Perhaps," he continued, "even the god in his kindness is offering to end my life not only at the right time, but also in the easiest way possible. For if I am condemned now, clearly I shall be able to die in the easiest way possible, according to the judgment of those who know about such matters, and with the least trouble to my friends, arousing in them the deepest longing for the dead. For when a man leaves behind nothing ugly or difficult in the minds of the living, and passes away while he is still sound in body and able to be cheerful in soul, this long-
8   ing necessarily arises. Rightly," he said, "the gods opposed my thinking about my defense at the very time when we thought we should try to get acquittal by every possible means. If I had succeeded in this, clearly, instead of preparing myself for ending my life now, I would have prepared myself for a miserable death in sickness or old age, where every kind of cheerless
9   suffering is concentrated.[2] By Zeus, Hermogenes," he added, "I am not eager for that. If I do annoy the jurors when I explain how many good things I think I have received from men and gods and the good opinion that I hold about myself, I shall prefer to die rather than to live without freedom because I pleaded to gain, in place of death, a much worse life."

10   Hermogenes said that this was what Socrates had decided when the prosecution accused him of not paying respect to the gods whom the state respects, and of introducing new

[2] Notice that Socrates speaks as if the death sentence had already been pronounced.

divinities and corrupting the young.[3] So Socrates stepped forward and spoke: "First of all, gentlemen, I am amazed at what   *11*
Meletus says. I do not pay respect to the gods the state respects? Meletus himself, if he had wished, as well as the rest
of those who happened by, could have seen me sacrificing
during public festivals at the public altars. As for the new   *12*
divinities, how is it introducing new divinities to say that the
voice of a god comes to me signifying what should be done?
Men who consult the cries of birds and the oracles of men
surely draw their conclusions from voices. Will anyone argue
that thunder does not speak or give the most weighty omens?
Doesn't the Pythian priestess [4] on the tripod report the messages from the god with her voice? At any rate the god has   *13*
foreknowledge of the future, foretelling it to whomever he
will; this is what everyone, including me, says and believes.
Some men call those who speak birds or voices or omens or
seers, but I speak of this as a *daimon,* and I think that by
naming it thus, I speak with more truth and holiness than
those who place the power of the gods in birds. I offer the
following proof that I am not lying against the god: I have
reported the advice of the god to many of my friends, and
I have never been shown to have lied." [5]

As they listened to these words, the jurors raised an uproar,   *14*
some because they did not believe what was said, others simply
because they envied Socrates, for he received more from the
gods than they. Again Socrates spoke: "Come, listen to some
more, so that those of you who so choose may strengthen your
disbelief in the fact that I am honored by divinities. Once
when Chaerephon, in the presence of many witnesses, asked at
Delphi about me, Apollo answered that no human being was
more free, more just, or more temperate than I." [6] Again, when   *15*

[3] The same text of the charge is given in *Recollections* I. 1. 1. In Plato's
Apology (24b) the charge listed third by Xenophon is put first.

[4] At the Oracle of Apollo at Delphi.

[5] The same argument is presented in *Recollections* I. 1. 3 ff., but in more
detail.

[6] In Plato's version in the *Apology* (21a), Chaerephon simply asks if
there is anyone wiser than Socrates. The oracle replied, "No!"

the jurors heard this, still more naturally, they raised an uproar. Socrates resumed speaking: "But gentlemen, the god has
spoken even greater oracles about Lycurgus the lawgiver of
Sparta than about me. It is said that as Lycurgus entered the
temple, the god said to him, 'I am considering whether to call
you god or man.' He did not liken me to a god, but he did
judge that I far excel men. Nevertheless, do not rashly believe
the god. Instead, investigate point by point what the god said.

16   Do you know anyone less a slave to the appetites of the body
than I? What man is freer than I, since I accept no gifts or
pay from anyone? Would you be reasonable to believe that
anyone is more just than a man so in harmony with the
present circumstances that he does not ask for anyone else's
possessions? How could anyone reasonably deny that I am
wise when, from the time I began to understand what was
said, I have never ceased to inquire into and learn whatever

17   good I could? Here, don't you think, is the proof that I have
not toiled in vain: many of the citizens who seek virtue, as
well as many foreigners, would rather be with me than with
anyone else. How shall we explain the fact that many men
seek to give me gifts, although everyone knows I have the
least money with which to repay them? What do you make of
the fact that no one asks me for favors, yet many acknowledge

18   that they owe me gratitude? How do you account for the fact
that during the siege [7] when others were feeling sorry for themselves, I was in no worse straits than when the state was at the
height of its prosperity; and that while others buy expensive
luxuries from the agora, I construct from the soul even more
pleasant products at no expense? If no one can convict me of
lying in all that I have just said about myself, isn't it just for

19   me to be praised by gods and men? In spite of this, Meletus,
do you say that I corrupt the young with such practices? Yet
surely we know what really corrupts the young. Tell me: do
you know someone who has been changed by me from a

[7] Lysander of Sparta besieged Athens in 404 B.C. at the end of the
Peloponnesian War.

reverent into an unholy man? From a prudent to an insolent man? From a frugal man to a spendthrift? From a light drinker to a drunkard, or from a hard worker to a man who is effeminate or dominated by some other evil pleasure? "

"By Zeus," said Meletus, "I know young men whom you   *20*
convinced to obey you instead of their parents! " [8]

"I acknowledge this in the question of education," replied Socrates, "for they know that I have been concerned with the question of education. In matters of health, men obey doctors, not their parents. In the assemblies all Athenians surely obey the men who speak most sensibly, not their relatives! Do you not also choose generals whom you believe to be wisest in military questions in preference to your fathers or your brothers or even, by Zeus! yourselves? "

"Socrates," replied Meletus, "it is profitable and customary   *21*
to do this."

"Then," said Socrates, "don't you think it amazing that in other activities, the experts should get not only an equal share, but even preference, but that I am being prosecuted by you on pain of death, even though I am judged by some to be an expert in the question of the greatest good to men, education? "

Clearly much more than this was said by Socrates, and by   *22*
his friends who joined in his defense. I have not, however, sought to relate everything about the trial. It was enough for me to demonstrate, first, that Socrates so conducted himself in everything that he did not appear either irreverent toward the gods or unjust toward men; and second, that he did not   *23*
think that he should plead not to die but that, instead, he thought it was time for him to die. That he had come to this conclusion became even more evident when the case was decided against him. First, when he was bidden to propose a counter-penalty, he would not do so or allow his friends to do so for him. He said that to propose a counter-penalty for

[8] This and the next sections appear to summarize *Recollections* I. 2. 49–55.

himself was to confess his guilt. Afterward, when his companions wanted to steal him from prison, he did not allow it.[9]
Indeed, he seemed to treat it as a joke, for he asked if they
knew a place, somewhere outside of Attica, where death did
not walk.

24   When the trial ended, we are told, Socrates said, "Gentlemen,
those who instructed the witnesses to perjure themselves by
bearing false witness against me, and those who were persuaded to do so, must be conscious within themselves of great
impiety and injustice. But as for me, why should I be less
proud now than before the sentence was passed, in view of the
fact that I have not been convicted of any of the charges they
brought against me? It has not been proven that I sacrifice to
any new divinities instead of to Zeus, Hera, and the other
gods with them; nor that I swear by new divinities, or respect
25   other gods. As for the young, how could I corrupt them by
training them in manliness and frugality? Not even the prosecution has alleged that I have done any of the crimes that
carry the death penalty, such as robbing a temple, stealing,
selling a free man into slavery, or betraying the state. Thus
I think it amazing that I have done a deed that appeared to
26   you to merit the death penalty. But nevertheless, I must not
be less proud because I die unjustly. That is a disgrace to
those who condemned me, not to me! Yet Palamedes, who
came to a similar end, consoles me. For still, even to this day,
he is honored with much more beautiful hymns than is
Odysseus, who unjustly slew him. I know that the future and
the past will testify that I never wronged anyone and never
made a man evil, and that I helped those who talked with me
by teaching them without taking any pay whatever good
I could."

27   After saying this, Socrates left in a manner suited to his
words, for his mien and bearing and step were radiant. When
he saw that the men who followed him had tears in their
eyes, he said, "What is this? Have you waited until now to
weep? Don't you know that long ago, when I was born, I was

[9] The account of his refusal to escape is given in Plato's *Crito*.

condemned to death by nature? If I am perishing prematurely while good is still abundant, clearly I and my friends must grieve. If I am ending life just as suffering is about to come, I think that all of you must rejoice at my good fortune."

A certain Apollodorus was present who loved Socrates 28 deeply, but was otherwise naïve. Apollodorus said, "But Socrates, the hardest thing for me to bear is to see you die unjustly." Socrates stroked the young man's head and said, "Dear Apollodorus, would you prefer to see me die justly?" As he spoke, he laughed.

It is said that when Socrates saw Anytus pass by, he said, 29 "That man is proud, as if he had done a great and noble act by putting me to death! And all because when I saw him deemed by the state to be worthy of the highest honors, I said that he ought not to educate his son in a tanning yard! What a villain he is!" continued Socrates. "He doesn't seem to realize which of us has performed the better and nobler deeds for the future, and is thus the real victor. Yet Homer has ascribed 30 to some who are about to die the power to know the future, and I, too, wish to prophesy.[10] Once for a short time I associated with Anytus' son, and I thought that his son was not weak in soul. So I told him not to stay in the slavish employment that his father had prepared for him. However, because he has no interested overseer, he will fall into some disgraceful habit and sink still deeper into depravity." In saying this 31 Socrates did not lie, for the young man indulged in wine and did not stop drinking day or night; in the end he became worthless to his state, his friends, and to himself. As for Anytus, because of the evil upbringing of his son and because of his lack of human feeling, even after his death he has ill repute.

Because Socrates praised himself, he aroused envy in court 32 and made the jurors all the more ready to condemn him. Yet I think he won a destiny that was dear to the gods, for he escaped the hardest part of life and he died the easiest form of

10 *Iliad* XVI. 851 ff., XXII. 358 ff.

33   death. He demonstrated the prowess of his soul; for when he decided that it was better for him to die than to continue to live, just as he never had opposed the other good things in life, he did not show weakness in the face of death, but *34*   received death cheerfully and paid his debt in full. As I think of Socrates' wisdom and nobility, I cannot fail to remember him, nor, upon remembering him, can I fail to praise him. If any of the men who pursue virtue has ever encountered anyone more helpful than Socrates, than man, I believe, has a right to be called the happiest man alive.

INDEX

The Library of Liberal Arts

SCHILLER, J., Wilhelm Tell

SCHLEGEL, J., On Imitation and Other Essays

SCHNEIDER, H., Sources of Contemporary Philosophical Realism in America

SCHOPENHAUER, A., On the Basis of Morality
Freedom of the Will

SELBY-BIGGE, L., British Moralists

SENECA, Medea
Oedipus
Thyestes

SHAFTESBURY, A., Characteristics

SHELLEY, P., A Defence of Poetry

SMITH, A., The Wealth of Nations (Selections)

Song of Roland, Terry, trans.

SOPHOCLES, Electra

SPIEGELBERG, H., The Socratic Enigma

SPINOZA, B., Earlier Philosophical Writings
On the Improvement of the Understanding

TERENCE, The Brothers
The Eunuch
The Mother-in-Law
Phormio
The Self-Tormentor
The Woman of Andros

Three Greek Romances, Hadas, trans.

TOLSTOY, L., What is Art?

VERGIL, Aeneid

VICO, G. B., On the Study Methods Our Time

VOLTAIRE, Philosophical Letters

WHITEHEAD, A., Interpretation of Science

WOLFF, C., Preliminary Discourse on Philosophy in General

XENOPHON, Recollections of Socrates *and* Socrates' Defense Before the Jury

THE AMERICAN HERITAGE SERIES

TOPICAL VOLUMES